THE
PRESENT STATE
OF
MUSIC
IN
GERMANY,
THE NETHERLANDS,
AND
UNITED PROVINCES.

O R,

The JOURNAL of a TOUR through those Countries, undertaken to collect Materials for

A GENERAL HISTORY OF MUSIC.

By CHARLES BURNEY, Muf. D.

IN TWO VOLUMES:

VOL. I.

Auf Virtuofen fep ftolj, Germanien, die du gezeiget;
In Frankreich und Welfchland find gröffere nicht.

Zacharià.

LONDON,

Printed for T. Becket and Co. Strand; J. Robson, New Bond-Street; and G. Robinson, Paternofter Row. 1773.

This is a facsimile of Charles Burney's The Present State of Music in Germany, the Netherlands, and the United Provinces, or, The Journal of a Tour through those Countries, undertaken to collect Materials for a General History of Music. London: Printed for T. Becket and Co. in the Strand; J. Robson, New Bond Street; and G. Robinson, Paternoster Row. 1773. This was the first edition. A second edition was published in 1775.

Dr. Charles Burney, Mus. D. (1726-1814), organist, composer and music historian.

Music related books written by Dr. Burney include:

1771:   The Present State of Music in France and Italy or, The Journal of a Tour through those Countries, undertaken to collect Materials for a General History of Music. London: Printed for T. Becket and Co. (Second edition 1773)

1771:   A Letter from the Late Signor Tartini to Signora Maddalena Lombardini (now Signora Sirmen). Published as an Important Lesson to Performers on the Violin. Translated by Dr. Burney. (Also 1779)

1773:   The Present State of Music in Germany, the Netherlands, and the United Provinces, or, The Journal of a Tour through those Countries, undertaken to collect Materials for a General History of Music. London: Printed for T. Becket and Co. 2 vols. (Second edition 1775)

1776-1789: A General History of Music from the Earliest Ages to the Present Period, to which is prefixed, a Dissertation on the Music of the Ancients. 4 vols. (Vol 1 reprinted in 1789).

1779   Account of an Infant Musician. [William Crotch.]

1785:   An account of Mademoiselle Theresa Paradis.

1785:   An Account of the Musical Performances in Westminster-Abbey, and the Pantheon, May 26th, 27th, 29th; and June the 3rd, and 5th, 1784. In Commemoration of Handel.

Standard works on the life of Dr. Burney include:
BURNEY, Frances ['Fanny', Madame d'Arblay, his daughter], Memoirs of Dr. Burney. (1832)
SCHOLES, Percy A.: The Great Dr. Burney: His Life, His Travels, His Works, His Family and His Friends.. (OUP, 1948)
LONSDALE, Roger: Dr. Charles Burney: A Literary Biography: (OUP, 1965)
More information, and fuller bibliography, can also be found in The New Grove Dictionary of Music and Musicians (Macmillan / OUP)

Reprinted 2008 Travis & Emery,
17 Cecil Court, London, WC2N 4EZ,
England.
(+44) 20 7240 2129
neworders@travis-and-emery.com
Bibliography – Travis & Emery ©2010

This work was published in two volumes.
Vol.1 Hardback 978-1-84955-064-2, Paperback 978-1-84955-065-9
Vol.2 Hardback 978-1-84955-066-6, Paperback 978-1-84955-067-3
Two vols in one book: Hardback 978-1-904331-57-5, Paperback 978-1-904331-58-2

THE

PRESENT STATE

OF

MUSIC

IN

GERMANY,

THE NETHERLANDS,

AND

UNITED PROVINCES.

OR,

The JOURNAL of a TOUR through thofe
Countries, undertaken to collect Materials for

A GENERAL HISTORY OF MUSIC.

By CHARLES BURNEY, Muf. D.

IN TWO VOLUMES.

VOL. I.

Auf Virtuofen fey ftolz, Germanien, die du gezeiget;
In Frankreich und Welfchland find gröffere nicht.

Zachariä.

LONDON,

Printed for T. BECKET and Co. Strand; J. ROBSON, New Bond-
Street; and G. ROBINSON, Paternofter Row. 1773.

INTRODUCTION.

IT is well known that such merchan-
dize as is capable of adulteration, is
seldom genuine after passing through
many hands; and this principle is still
more generally allowed with respect to
intelligence, which is, perhaps, never
pure but at the source.

Music has, through life, been the favourite object of my pursuit, not only
with respect to the practice of it as a
profession, but the history of it as an art;
and that my knowledge might be free
from such falshood and error as the
plainest and simplest facts are known to

gather

gather up in fucceffive relations, I have made a fecond tour on the continent, taking nothing upon report, of which I could procure better teftimony, and, accumulating the moft authentic memorials of the times that are paft; and as I have, in a late publication, endeavoured to do juftice to the talents and attainments of the prefent muficians of France and Italy, I fhall now make the fame attempt with refpect to thofe of Germany, hoping that the teftimony of one who has himfelf been witnefs of the particulars he relates, will have a weight which integrity itfelf cannot give to hear-fay evidence, and that the mind of the reader will be more entertained, in proportion as it is more fatisfied of the truth of what is written. For if *knowledge* be *medicine for the foul,* according to the famous infcription on the Alexandrian Library *, it feems as much to concern us to obtain it genuine, as to procure unadulterated medicine for the body.

---

[v]

Travelling for information concerning
the tranfactions of remote countries, was
much more practifed by the writers of
antiquity than it has been by thofe of
later times, who have found it more convenient to compile books at their own
fire-fide, from books which have been
compiled before, than to crofs feas,
mountains, and deferts, in foreign countries, to feek for new and authentic materials. But Homer, Herodotus, Plato,
Plutarch, and Paufanias, who were great
travellers, either lived in times when
there were few books to confult, or, if
they were not poffeffed of more wealth
than modern authors, muft have met with
more than modern hofpitality ; for long
voyages, however neceffary, would otherwife have been fcarcely practicable.

For my part, who have travelled without thefe advantages, and who pretend
not to the character of *fage*, if it be faid,
that the object of my purfuit is by no
means

means equivalent to my labour and expence ; I can only anfwer, that though I
am unwilling to allow the knowledge of
a fcience which diffufes fo much blame-
lefs pleafure, through a circle of fuch vaft
extent, to be of fmall importance, yet I
moft fincerely wifh that I could have procured it upon eafier terms, and have vifited remote countries after the delibe-
rate and parfimonious manner of Afcle-
piades, who, according to Tertullian,
made the tour of the world on a cow's
back, and lived upon her milk.

It is however certain, that whatever
will juftify my rambling through France
and Italy after the *materia mufica*, or apo-
logize for it, may with the fame force
and propriety be pleaded for my having
vifited Germany ; for though Italy has
carried *vocal* mufic to a perfection unknown in any other country, much of
the prefent excellence of *inftrumental* is
certainly owing to the natives of Germany,

many, as wind and keyed inftruments
have never, perhaps, in any age or country, been brought to a greater degree of
refinement, either in conftruction or ufe,
than by the modern Germans.

The notice and affiftance with which I
was honoured by feveral perfons of diftinction on the continent, are acknowledged in the courfe of my narrative;
but to avoid repetitions in my book, and
to follow an impulfe of gratitude, perhaps not unmixed with vanity, I muft
here declare, that for thefe and many
other advantages which my journey produced, I am principally indebted to the
patronage of the Earl of Sandwich, who,
to affift me in calling the attention of the
public to the hiftory of his favourite art,
and in recording the talents of its moft
illuftrious profeffors in remote countries,
was pleafed to honour me with recommendatory letters, in his own hand, to
every nobleman and gentleman of this
coun-

country who refided in a public character in the feveral cities through which I paff-ed; the influence of which was fo power-ful as to gain me eafy accefs to thofe who were not only the moft able, but whom I was fo fortunate as to find the moft will-ing to forward my undertaking.

THE

PRESENT STATE

OF

MUSIC, &c.

St. OMERS.

I Muft confefs, that my appetite for French mufic was not very keen when I now landed on the continent, July 6th, 1772. However, being detained at St. Omers a day longer than I expected, I vifited fome of the churches there, as well as the theatre; but heard nothing in either which inclined me to change my fentiments concerning the national tafte of France, for mufic.

B   A com-

A company of ſtrolling players, from
Dunkirk, acted, on the night of my arrival, a tragedy and a comedy. I went to
the playhouſe, which I found ſmall and
dirty; and though the tragedy was half
over when I arrived, there was no other
company in the boxes, than two or three
Engliſh families, and a few of the
officers of the garriſon. It is impoſſi ble
for Engliſhmen to judge, accurately, of
French acting, and declamation; but
theſe performers ſeemed much more at
their eaſe, and appeared more like the
characters they were to repreſent, than
thoſe on the Engliſh ſtage, who, except
a few of the principal actors, are generally ſo aukward and unnatural, as to
deſtroy all illuſion.

At the cathedral of St. Omer there
is a very fine ſixteen feet organ, which is
played in a maſterly, but old ſtyle, by a
prieſt, father Thomas, who teaches the
harpſichord to many Engliſh people, as
well as other inhabitants of that city.

But

But the moſt conſiderable inſtrument there, in figure and grandeur, is the organ at the abbey of St. Bertin: it was built but five years ago, by a country mechanic, who could neither write, read, nor play on his inſtrument when it was made. I had, as yet, ſeen nothing ſo elegant and magnificent as the caſe and ornaments of this organ; the ſtops are numerous, and the movements light and tolerably quiet; there are pedals, but there is no ſwell, or great variety in the ſolo ſtops, nor do I think the tone ſo ſweet as that of the cathedral. But the beſt organ in this part of the world, for ſweetneſs of tone, is an old one at the monaſtery of Clairmarais, about a league from St. Omers. The organiſt there is a friar; and that of the abbey of St. Bertin is a nephew and ſcholar of father Thomas.

There is a little organ, called a *poſi-tif*, conſiſting of four ſtops only, in the chancel of the abbey, which is uſed on

com-

common occafions; it is nearly fuch a one
as I remember to have feen and heard
Colifta play upon, to accompany the
voices, at the church of St. John La-
teran, at Rome, in 1770.

At mounting guard in the *Grande Place*
of St. Omer, I obferved that the *fer-*
pent was ufed in the military band, as
a double bafe to a great number of baffoons, horns, and hautboys, and had a
very good effect.

L I S L E.

To perfons who ftay but a fhort time
in French garrifoned towns, the military
affords confiderable amufement; there
are not at prefent above four batta-
lions, or two thoufand men, quartered
in the city; though it is ufual for the
garrifon to confift of ten thoufand. The
mounting guard upon the *Grande Place,*
or fquare, is, in itfelf, a gay and entertaining fight; yet it always gives
me a melancholy, and painful fenfation,

[5]

to see the people out-numbered by the military. So many stout and robust fellows kept from the plough, and from manufactures, must be a great burden upon the community, and totally useless in time of peace, to any thing but ambitious and oppressive views.

Having visited this city, in quest of musical information, so lately as the year 1770, I expected to find nothing new, that was very interesting; however, I attended to the military music, which is much changed here since I was last in France. The marches, as well as musicians, are chiefly German. The *crotolo* is used here as I had seen it at Florence; it serves very well to mark the time in marching, though it has only one tone, like that of a side drum: it is the same instrument as that which the ancients called the *cymbalum*. The Turks were the first among the moderns who used it in their troops; the form

B 3

is

is that of a bafon, or the cover to a
difh ; there is one for each hand. It is
made of brafs, but the vibration is fo
ftopt by its being in contact with the
hand, that it cannot be called fonorous,
it is rather a clafhing than a founding
inftrument of percuffion ; however, its
effect in marking the time is fo powerful as to be diftinctly heard through
the ftunning noife of forty drums.

In fpeaking of military mufic, it
feems not unworthy of remark, that
drums, *monotonous* as they are, frequently play in *two parts*. I obferved
to-day, at mounting guard, that, of forty
drums which began to beat together
ifochronous, or in equal time, one half
continued to beat the march, and the
other half accompanied them with a
continual roll for feveral bars: the effect
of this is admirable, as it contributes to
animate the troops, without deftroying
or altering the divifion of time, by
which they are to meafure their fteps.

In

In other mufic, during a long note, which is either fimply fuftained in a fwell, or *diminuendo,* or has a continued fhake, the time is wholly unmarked, unlefs its accents and proportions are pointed out and regulated by fome other part; a fingle drum, while one hand rolls, has frequently the time marked by the fingle ftrokes of the other, given at ftated periods. The ufe of mufic, in marching, as well as in dancing, is more to mark the fteps than delight the ear; and the beft inftruments, perhaps, for both purpofes, are the drum and tabor, neither of which has more than one found.

After Moliere's *Ecole des Maris,* I heard here *l'Amitié à l'Epreuve,* taken from one of the *Contes Moraux* of Marmontel, by Favart, with *ariettes* by Gretry: the mufic is full of pretty things, and it is an honour to the French to admire the compofitions of this ingenious compofer, who feems, in

gratitude,

gratitude, to conform, as much as he can, to the national tafte; though his melodies are more frequently Italian than French, and his modulation and accompaniments are new and pleafing. To criticife the execution of this pretty opera would be firing at carrion crows, not worth powder and fhot. But in this fevere cenfure I muft diftinguifh the actors from the fingers, and the voices from the corruption and abufe of them.

Both the pieces were well acted; but, as to *finging*, nothing could be more offenfive; and yet there was not one bad voice among the performers: one of the young actreffes had, indeed, a voice that was fweetly toned, and of great compafs; but the fongs were too difficult for her execution, and fhe joined to the national falfe direction of voice, to forcing, fcreaming, and bad tafte, that incurable and infufferable expreffion, which is equally difgufting to the learned and the ignorant of other countries.

In

In travelling through French Flanders, I could not help obferving that the finging of the common people is ftrongly tinctured with the *plain-chant*, which they hear fo frequently at church. All the labouring people and *bourgeois* go to matins as foon as it is light on common days, and on Sundays and feftivals two or three times in the courfe of the day; fo that by their conftantly hearing the priefts, and finging with them, they acquire that kind of melody and expreffion which is ufed in the church, and apply it to their fongs, in their work-fhops, and in the ftreet.

Though I omitted no opportunity of hearing all the inftruments and performers I could, in my way through French Flanders, yet they furnifhed no new ideas or reflections concerning either the tafte, or ftyle, of French muficians. To defcribe them, therefore, would be only to repeat what I have already faid on the fubject, in my former mufical tour

through

through this country. I muſt, however
allow, and it would diſcover a total
want of candour to be ſilent on the ſubject, that upon keyed inſtruments, particularly the harpſichord, the French, in
point of neatneſs, preciſion, and brilliancy of execution, are not excelled by
the people of any other country in Europe ; and it is but juſt to obſerve likewiſe, that the French military muſic
is now not only much better in itſelf,
but better performed than it was a few
years ago : and a very intelligent Engliſh officer, who was with me on the
parade, remarked the ſame improvement in the diſcipline, dreſs, and appearance of the French troops in the
ſame ſpace of time. The men are now
ſelect, the manœuvres ſhortened, and
there is ſome appearance both of the
gentleman and the ſoldier, even in the
common men.

COUR-

COURTRAY.

When I arrived at this place, which is the firſt conſiderable town in the Auſtrian Netherlands, I found a remarkable change in the language, manners, and muſic of the people. It is very embarraſſing to a ſtranger to find within the compaſs of a hundred Engliſh miles, four languages very different from each other: French, Flemiſh, Walloon, and Low Dutch. At Courtray, the common people ſpeak the Walloon language: I accoſted ſeveral in the ſtreets, in French, but they did not underſtand me; ſo that the Abbé du Bos' aſſertion, and the conſequence he draws from it, that French is the univerſal language of the Flemings, fall to the ground, for it is a common thing, even at Liſle, for two people to converſe in two different languages; the inhabitant of Liſle aſks the country-man, who comes to market,

the

the price of his commodities in French, and is anfwered in Flemifh; and both underftand each other's dialect, though unable to fpeak it.

In the town of Courtray, the organ, at the collegiate church of *Notre Dame*, is difpofed of in a very fingular manner; it is placed in a gallery at the weft end of the building; but, in order to pre-ferve the window, which was neceffary to light the body of the church, the organ is divided in two parts, one of which is fixed on one fide of the win-dow, and one on the other; the bel-lows run under the window, and com-municate with both parts of the inftru-ment, which is a large one of fixteen feet, with pedals, and feems to have been but lately erected. The keys are in the middle, under the window, but not to be feen below; the choir is accom-panied, even when the organ does not play, with a *ferpent*, as at Paris, and a double bafe, as at Rome. It was in
this

this town that I firſt perceived the paſſion for *carillons*, or chimes, which is
ſo prevalent throughout the Netherlands. I happened to arrive at eleven
o'clock, and half an hour after the
chimes played a great number of chearful tunes, in different keys, which awakened my curioſity for this ſpecies of muſic
ſo much, that, when I came to

G H E N T,

I determined to inform myſelf, in a
particular manner, concerning the *carillon* ſcience. For this purpoſe, I mounted
the town belfrey, from whence I had a
full view, not only of the city of Ghent,
which is reckoned one of the largeſt in
Europe, but could examine the mecha-
niſm of the chimes, as far as they are
played by clock-work, and likewiſe ſee
the *Carilloneur* perform with a kind of
keys communicating with bells, as thoſe
of the harpſichord and organ do with
ſtrings and pipes.

I ſoon

[14]

I foon found that the chimes in
thefe countries had a greater number of bells than thofe of the largeft
peal in England; but, when I mounted
the belfrey, I was aftonifhed at the
great quantity of bells I faw; in fhort,
there is a complete feries or fcale of
tones and femitones, like thofe on the
harpfichord and organ. The *Caril-
lonur* was literally *at work*, and *hard
work* indeed it muft be; he was in his
fhirt with the collar unbuttoned, and in
a violent fweat. There are pedals communicating with the great bells, upon
which, with his feet, he played the
bafe to feveral fprightly and rather
difficult airs, performed with the two
hands upon the upper fpecies of keys.
Thefe keys are projecting fticks, wide
enough afunder to be ftruck with violence and velocity by either of the
two hands edge ways, without the danger of hitting the neighbouring keys.
The player has a thick leather covering
for

for the little finger of each hand, otherwife it would be impoffible for him to
fupport the pain which the violence of
the ftroke neceffary to be given to
each key, in order to its being diftinctly heard throughout a very large
town, requires.

The *carillons* are faid to be originally of
Aloft, in this country, and are ftill here,
and in Holland, in their greateft perfection. It is certainly a Gothic invention,
and perhaps a barbarous tafte, which neither the French, the Englifh, nor the Italians have imitated or encouraged. The
Carilloneur, at my requeft, played feveral pieces very dexteroufly, in three
parts, the firft and fecond treble with
the two hands on the upper fet of
keys, and the bafe with the feet on
the pedals.

The *Carilloneur* plays four times a
week, Sunday, Monday, Wednefday,
and Friday, from half an hour paft
eleven till twelve o'clock: it is conftant

2   employment

employment for a watch or clock-maker
to attend the works of the common
chimes ; here he has an apartment under the belfrey, and it is by him
that the *Carilloneur* is paid. This place
and Antwerp are, according to the
inhabitants, the moſt celebrated cities
in the Netherlands, and perhaps in the
world, for carillons and chimes.

The great convenience of this kind
of muſic is, that it entertains the inhabitants of a whole town, without giving
them the trouble of going to any particular ſpot to hear it ; but the want of
ſomething to ſtop the vibration of each
bell, at the pleaſure of the player,
like the valves of an organ, and
the red cloth in the jacks of a harpſichord, is an intolerable defect to a
cultivated ear : for by the notes of one
paſſage perpetually running into another, every thing is rendered ſo inar-
ticulate and confuſed as to occaſion
a very diſagreeable jargon. As to
the

the clock-work chimes, or thofe worked by a barrel, nothing, to my thinking, can be more tirefome; for, night and day, to hear the fame tune played every hour, during fix months, in fuch a ftiff and unalterable manner, requires that kind of patience, which nothing but a total abfence of tafte can produce.

As Ghent was the firft town which I had been in, that had a German garrifon in it, or, rather, troops in the pay, and under the difcipline of Germany, I was curious to hear the military mufic. I found two Walloon regiments here; and though no general officer was on the fpot, yet there were two bands attending every morning and evening, on the *Place d'Armes,* or parade. The one was an extra-band of profeffed muficians, confifting of two hautbois, two clarinets, two baffoons, and two French horns; the other were enlifted men and boys, belonging to the regiments; the number of thefe amount-ed to twenty. There were four trum-

C pets,

[18]

pets, three fifes, two hautbois, two
clarinets, two *tambours de basque*, two
French horns, one *crotolo*, or cymbal,
three fide-drums, and one great kettle-
drum.   All thefe fonorous inftruments,
in the open air, have a very animating and
pleafing effect.

I foon found, in vifiting the churches
of this country, that fplitting an organ in twain, in order to preferve a
window, was no uncommon thing.   At
the Jefuit's church, for Jefuits have
ftill an exiftence here, there is a fmall
organ, for this country, placed in a gallery
at the weft window, divided in that manner.   I found but one fet of keys, from
C, to G, no pedals, and but few
ftops, the tone was coarfe and noify
when heard near, but, by the fize and
conftruction of the building, it was fo
foftened and meliorated, as to found very
agreeably, at a diftance.

At the great church of St. Bavo, two
ferpents and a double bafe accompany the
chant,

chant, when fung in parts, even when the organ is not played. The organ here is placed under the arch of the left-fide aile, at the entrance into the choir, in order to preferve the center, or broad aile, from being interfected with an organ-loft, which frequently deftroys all the fymmetry and proportions of a building; as an organ, when placed over the weft door, frequently darkens the whole church, by fhutting up a principal window, originally intended for other purpofes, by the architect, than mere external ornament.

I did not quit Ghent without vifiting the principal libraries there, in hopes of meeting with ancient manufcript mufic, which might afcertain the affertion of Lod. Guicciardini, that counter-point took its rife, and was firft cultivated in Flanders; but I neither found at the abbey of St. Peter (the oldeft and richeft in Flanders) nor at the Auguftines, or

C 2

Domi-

Dominicans, where the libraries are very confiderable, any thing to my purpofe.

A L O S T.

Here I found, in the church of St. Martin, a noble organ, built by Van Petigham, and fon, of Ghent, but five years fince, which fills the whole weft end of the church ; its form is elegant, and the ornaments are in a good tafte. It has fifty-three ftops, three fets of keys, great organ, choir organ, and echo, down to F, on the fourth line in the bafe *. The touch is not fo heavy as might be expected from the great refiftance of fuch a column of air as is necefiary for fo confiderable a number of ftops. The reed ftops are well toned, the diapafons well voiced, and the effect of the whole chorus rich and noble : I was the more particular in my obfervations upon this inftrument, in order to enable myfelf to compare its contents with thofe of the large organs

* The pedals went down two octaves lower.

organs which I expected to fee hereafter in Holland and Germany. The French organ-builders are much efteemed by the Germans themfelves, for the fimplicity of their movements, and the mechanifm of the whole; but the variety which thefe ftops afford is not proportioned to their number; we have frequently more folo ftops in an Englifh organ of half the fize and price ; however, Silbermann, the moft celebrated organbuilder in Germany, who died not long ago, refided and worked many years in France, from whence he brought feveral improvements in the conftruction of organs, that he afterwards applied to thofe which he erected in his own country.

The voices in the church at Aloft are accompanied, befides the organ, with fix or eight inftruments every day, and on feftivals by a great band ; and the mufical fafte here, as far as I could judge by the

per-

performance of the organift and his fon, is more Italianifed, or at leaft Germanif-ed, than in any of the churches of France.

B R U S S E L S.

The theatre in this city is one of the moft elegant I ever faw, on this fide the Alps; it is conftructed in the Italian manner; there are five rows of boxes, nineteen in each, which, feverally, contain fix perfons in front. There are feats in the pit, five or fix of which are railed off for the accommodation of ftrangers, who, otherwife, would be in danger of obtaining no good places, as the boxes are ufually let to fubfcribers, and there are no galleries.

The orcheftra of this theatre is celebrated all over Europe. It is, at prefent, under the direction of M. Fitzthumb, a very active and intelligent *maeftro di capella*, who beats the time, and is indefatigable

fatigable in preferving good difcipline, and M. Vanmaldere, brother of the compofer of that name, whofe fymphonies are well known in England. M. Vanmaldere, fince the death of his brother, plays the principal violin, though the violoncello is his inftrument.

The piece that was performed to night, July 15th, 1772, was *Zemire* and *Azor*, a fpecies of *Comedie larmoyante*, written by M. Marmontel, and fet by M. Gretry; it is interfperfed with airs and dances. As the drama is French, the performance was after the French manner, and confequently fubject to much criticifm. As an opera, it might be divided into the following conftituent parts: *Poetry, Mufic, Singing, Acting, Dancing, Orcheftra, Theatre, Scenes,* and *Decorations;* and, it is but juftice to fay, that, of thefe, a great majority were good; however, let us difcriminate, for to judge a performance of this kind in the grofs, by faying that the whole was very good, bad, or in-

C 4   different,

different, would be unjuft as well as
taftelefs. The fubject of the *Poetry* is
a fairy tale, which is wrought into an
interefting drama with great art, tafte,
and genius; and is wholly worthy of
its elegant and refined author. If it were,
however, permitted to doubt of the perfection of particular parts of the production of fo able a writer, it might
perhaps be faid that fome of the fongs
contain too many words and ideas for
a fimplicity of air, if compared with
thofe of Metaftafio, the true model of
perfection in this particular; it alfo ftruck
me, as an impropriety, for the daughter of a great Perfian merchant to fing
two or three duets with her father's
flave. Several parts of the piece too are
made to be fung, which fhould, in this
kind of drama, be declaimed, particularly in the laft fcene of the firft act.

The *Mufic* of this opera, is, in general,
admirable; the overture is fpirited and
full of effects; the ritornels, and other

pieces

pieces of fymphony, are full of new
ideas and imagery; now and then, indeed, with the affiftance of the finging,
the airs bordered too much on the old
ftyle of French mufic. However, the
melody is more frequently Italian than
French, and the accompaniments are
both rich, ingenious, and tranfparent, if
I may be allowed the expreffion, by
which I mean, that the air is not fuf-
focated, but can be diftinctly heard
through them.

The *Singing* may be pronounced to have
been but indifferent: there were three male
and three female voices employed, no one
of which was good, and out of the whole
number, not one had either a fhake, or
the faculty of finging in tune; at beft,
they would have been called in England,
only pretty ballad-fingers. One of the
females, Defoix, who performed the part
of *Zemire*, had fomething like execution,
and a compafs of voice; yet, with thefe
advantages, her performance was unfteady
and unfinifhed.

The

The *Acting* was, in general, charming, full of propriety and grace.

The *Dancing* was below criticifm.

The *Orcheftra* was admirably conducted, and the band, taken as a whole, was numerous, powerful, correct, and attentive: but, in its feparate parts, the horns were bad, and out of tune; which was too difcoverable in the capital fong of the piece, when they were placed at different diftances from the audience, to imitate an echo, occafioned by the rocks, in a wild and defert fcene. The firft clarinet, which ferved as a hautboy, was, though a very good one, too fharp the whole night; and the bafes, which were all placed at one end of the orcheftra, played fo violently, that it was more like the rumbling reverberation of thunder, than mufical found. The four double bafes, employed in this band were too powerful for the reft of the inftruments. There was no harpfichord, which, as there were but two pieces of recitative, and thofe accompanied, was perhaps not wanted.

The

The *Theatre* has been defcribed above, and I have only to add, that it is lofty and noble; but though conftructed much after the Italian model, it is far inferior in fize to moft of the theatres of Italy. The *Scenes* and *Decorations* were rich, ingenious, and elegant.

July 16. This evening, after a pretty comedy, by Boiffy, called *le Mercure Galant*, the *Huron* was very well acted, though poorly fung. However, the little Defoix, who did the part of Zemire laft night, was much more at her eafe now, as all her fongs were fuch as fuited her powers. She is rather lefs French in her manner of finging than the reft; but fhe is ignorant of mufic, and a Frenchwoman, no trivial objections to her finging well.

The method of playing the march in this piece had a very fine effect, by the judicious ufe of the *Crefcendo* and *Diminuendo*. It was begun behind the fcenes, at the end of the ftage, fo foft as to be

I   fcarcely

fcarcely heard; and after the band had gradually approached the audience, and were arrived at the greateft degree of force, they retired in the fame flow manner, infenfibly diminifhing the found to the laft audible degree of *Piano*.

ANTWERP.

It was in this city, that I expected to meet with materials the moft important to the hiftory of counter-point, or mufic in different parts, as it was here, according to Lodovico Guicciardini, and, after him, feveral others, who took the fact upon truft, that moft of the great Flemifh muficians, who fwarmed all over Europe in the fixteenth century, were bred. I arrived here Friday evening, July 17th: it is a city that fills the mind with more melancholy reflections concerning the viciffitudes of human affairs, and the tranfient ftate of worldly glory, than any other in modern times: the exchange, which

which ferved as a model to Sir Th. Gref-
ham, when he built that of London, and
which, though ftill intire, is as ufelefs to
the inhabitants, as the *Colofeo* at Rome:
TheTown-houfe, conftructed as a tribunal,
for the magiftrates, at the head of two
hundred thoufand inhabitants, which are
now reduced to lefs than twenty thoufand : the churches, the palaces, the
fquares, and whole ftreets, which, not two
hundred years ago, were fcarce fufficient
to contain the people for whom they
were defigned, and which are now almoft
abandoned : the fpacious and commodious quays, the numerous canals, cut
with fuch labour and expence, the noble
river Schelde, wider than the Thames
at Chelfea-reach, which ufed to be covered with fhips from all quarters of the
world, and on which now, fcarce a fifhing
boat can be difcovered : all contribute
to point out the inftability of fortune,
and to remind us that, what Babylon,

Car-

Carthage, Athens, and Palmyra now are, the moſt flouriſhing cities of the preſent period, muſt, in the courſe of time, inevitably become!

The cathedral of *Notre Dame*, except the choir, was deſtroyed by fire, in the year 1533, as a great part of Rome was in 1527, which renders it difficult to find any manuſcript muſic of anterior times, in either of theſe cities.

It was rebuilt again the year following, more beautifully than ever, and is eſteemed ſuperior to all the Gothic buildings of this country, eſpecially the ſteeple, which is extremely light and elegant. The church was, however, pillaged and much defaced in 1560 by the *Iconoclaſts,* or image breakers, as the Dutch rebels, or heretics, are called; but ever ſince the year 1584, when it was taken by the duke of Parma, it has continued to be enriched with ſuperb altars and monuments, together with paintings by the firſt maſters;

ters; it is five hundred feet long, two hundred and forty wide, and three hundred and sixty high, and is supported by a hundred and twenty-five pillars; it was first built in the thirteenth century. The emperor Charles V. laid the first stone of the present choir. In 1521 the chapter of canons was instituted by Godfrey of Boulogne, king of Jerusalem; their number at first was only twelve, but it is now twenty-four; there are eight minor canons, with a number of chaplains, &c. which altogether form an assembly in the choir, to the amount of seventy beneficed clergy. There are three organs in this church, one very large, on the right hand side, at the west end of the choir, and a small one in a a chapel on each side the broad aile.

The organist at present is M. Vanden Bosch, he is a spirited and masterly player. The chanting here, as in other churches of this country, is accompanied

by

by the double bafe and *ferpent ;* an excellent fervice was fung on Saturday afternoon, July, 18th, out of a printed book,
which had for title, *Octo Cantica Divæ
Mariæ Virginis, fecundum Octo Modos,
Auctore Arturo Aux-Couteaux,* Parifiis,
1641.

At the Jefuit's college, I was treated
with great politenefs, and affifted in my
refearches by the learned father Gefquiere, together with father Newton and
brother Blithe, two Englifhmen of that
college. The former fhewed me a manufcript treatife on mufic, which, from
the kind of writing, is judged to be nine
hundred years old; and a fine ancient manufcript of our famous *Magna Charta;*
both of which feem to have come from
England, or at leaft to have been in the
poffeffion of an Englifhman, as there is
the fignature of *John Cotton* in both.

At the Dominicans church, there are
two organs, which are efteemed the beft
in

in the town; the one is very large, with
pedals, fifty-four ftops, and three entire
fets of keys, from C to c; it was built
in 1654. I found the pipes of thefe inftruments well toned, but fo miferably
out of tune, as to give more pain
than pleafure to the hearer. One of the
four monkifh organifts who attended
me in a very obliging manner, pleaded
poverty upon this occafion, and faid, they
could afford to have their inftruments put
in order but feldom, on account of the
expence.

As no picture worth looking at here,
is fhewn to a ftranger, without a *Schelling*
or two, a curtain being placed before each,
which *Simony* only can draw, I afked, not
indeed with much expectation that it would
be taken, whether I might venture to tender
any thing to the venerable perfon above-
mentioned, and, upon an anfwer in the
affirmative, I made my humble offering,
which was, as elfewhere, received with
great good nature and condefcenfion.

D   Sunday,

Sunday, 19th. I this morning at feven o'clock attended the firft mafs. There were a few violins, two baffoons, and a double bafe placed with the voices in the organ-loft, over the weft door of the choir; but before thefe were employed, a confiderable part of the fervice was chanted in *Canto Fermo*, with only a *ferpent*, and two baffoons in accompaniment; and, afterwards, the voices and inftruments in the organ-loft performed the ufual fervices in three or four parts, I mean voice parts, with inftruments. However, the fmall number of violins, in fo large a building, and thofe not of the firft clafs, had but a mean effect.

At nine o'clock high mafs began, and continued upwards of two hours. I attended this in the choir, in different parts of the church, and in the organ-loft, to hear the mufic, and its effects, at different diftances, and in different fituations; but I found none which pleafed me. The performances to which I had been accuftomed in Italy,

Italy, and, indeed, in the choirs of London,
were greatly fuperior to this. Whatever
merit the Antwerpians may have had,
in furpaffing the reft of Europe, in arts,
fciences, and commerce, two hundred
years ago, they certainly have no claim
to pré-eminence now; no part of their
ancient grandeur is vifible at prefent, but
in the church : there, indeed, riches,
fplendor, and expence are ftill as con-
fpicuous as ever, though but a fmall part
of this expence is appropriated to mufic.
The church revenues are applied to the
maintenance of the feveral orders of the
clergy; to that almoft innumerable quantity of wax-lights, for ever burning, and to
thofe fumptuous veftments, and tawdry
ornaments, with which they dazzle the
eyes of the multitude ; but as for mufic,
they have been fo long accuftomed to
inaccurate and flovenly execution, that
they feem to have loft all diftinction. I
did not meet with one fingle organ in
the whole town that was in tune; and

as

as to the few violins employed in the church, they are mere fcrapers. The baffoons, players in common ufe, are worfe than thofe nocturnal performers, who, in London, walk the ftreets during winter, under the denomination of *Waits*; and for the *ferpent*, it is not only over-blown, and deteftably out of tune, but exactly refembling in tone, that of a great hungry, or rather angry, Effex calf.

Before the fervice in the choir began with the organ, the canons and boys marched in proceffion round the church, with each a lighted taper in his hand, chanting the pfalms, in four parts, with the two baffoons, and *ferpent* above-mentioned; but all was fo diffonant and falfe, that notwithftanding the building is immenfe, and very favourable to found, which it not only augments, but meliorates, and in fpite of two or three fweet and powerful voices among the boys, the whole was intolerable to me, who remained in the choir, from whence I expected to enjoy

enjoy the natural *Diminuendo* and *Cref-cendo,* of a large body of found retreating and advancing by fuch flow degrees.

While that part of the fervice, which fucceeded this proceffion, was performing, I went up into the organ-loft, and was very politely treated by the organift, M. Vanden Bofch, who is a man of confiderable merit in his profeffion ; his ftyle of playing is modern, and he is very dexterous in the ufe of the pedals *. This inftrument of *Notre Dame,* contains upwards of fifty ftops, and has a full compafs; it has been built about a hun-

* When I ufe the epithets *old* and *new,* I mean neither as a term of reproach, or ftigma, but merely to tell the reader in what ftyle a piece is conceived, or written ; and he will fuppofe it to be better or worfe, as he pleafes. In Italy, though an old opera is as ufelefs and neglected as an almanac of laft year, yet an old compofition, if it be the beft of the time in which it was made, I fhall always fpeak of with refpect ; but as to *Performance,* an old fafhioned manner, whether the confequence of ignorance or obftinacy, will not, perhaps, be treated with equal indulgence.

D 3

dred

dred and fifty years, and would be well toned, if it were in tune.

After church, I went home with M. Vanden Bofch, who was fo obliging as to fhew me his inftruments and books. Several compofitions for the harpfichord of this mafter, have been engraved at Paris; he has a very good tafte, and great fire, both in writing and playing.

In my refearches after old mufic in this place, I was directed to Monf. ——— the finging mafter of St. James's church, a Frenchman. Indeed, I was obligingly conducted to his houfe, by one of the canons, and upon my acquainting him with my errand, and afking him the queftion I had before put to all the muficians, and men of learning that I had met with in France and Italy, without obtaining much fatisfaction, " *where, and* " *when did counter-point, or modern har-* " *mony begin?*" the Abbé's anfwer was quick, and firm. " O Sir, counter-point " was certainly invented in France."

" But,

" But, faid I, L. Guicciardini, and the
" Abbé du Bos, give it to the Flamands."
This made no kind of impreffion on my
valiant Abbé, who ftill referred me to
France for materials to afcertain the fact.
" But, Sir, faid I, What part of France
" muft I go to; I have already made all
" poffible enquiry in that kingdom, and
" had the honour of being every day
" permitted to fearch in the *Bibliotheque*
" *du Roi*, at Paris, for more than a
" month together, in hopes of finding
" fomething to my purpofe, but in vain;
" and as you were in poffeffion of the
" old manufcript mufic belonging to your
" church, I was inclined to believe it
" poffible, that you could have pointed
" out to me fome compofitions, which,
" if not the *firft* that were made in
" counter-point, would at leaft, be more
" ancient than thofe which I had found
" elfewhere." " *Mais, Monf. foyez fure que*
" *tout cela étoit inventé en France.*" This
was all the anfwer I could get, and upon

my

my preffing him to tell me where I might be furnifhed with proofs of this affertion, *Ah, ma foi, je n'en fais rien,* was his whole reply. I had been for fome time preparing for a retreat from this ignorant coxcomb, by fhuffling towards the door, but after this I flew to it as faft as I could, firft making my bow, and affuring him, fincerely, that I was extremely forry to have given him fo much trouble.

In the afternoon I attended vefpers at the church of our Lady; there were rather more inftrumental performers than in the morning, but all of the fame kind, as to excellence. The refponfes in the cathedral here, and indeed in all the other churches of Flanders, where inftruments are employed, are made in four vocal parts; but the inftrumental performers flourifh and fcrape with as much violence as at our theatre, when Richard the Third enters, or the king of Denmark caroufes; which, in my opinion, betrays a barbarous tafte, and total want of decency. The
only

only entertainment I received from the whole mufic, was that which the long voluntary afforded me, which M. Vanden Bofch was fo obliging as to play, at my requeft, after church, in which he difplayed great abilities.

After this I went to a very large building on a quay, at the fide branch of the Scheld, which is called the *Oofters Huys,* or Eafterlings houfe; it was formerly ufed as a ware-houfe by the merchants trading to Lubec, Hamburg, and the Hanfeatic towns; it is a very handfome ftructure, and has ferved, in time of war, as a barrack for two thoufand men. I fhould not have mentioned my vifiting this building, if I had not found in it a large quantity of mufical inftruments of a peculiar conftruction. There are between thirty and forty of the common-flute kind, but differing in fome particulars; having, as they increafe in length, keys and crooks, like hautbois and baffoons; they were made at Hamburg,

and

and are all of one fort of wood, and by
one maker; CASPER RAVCHS SCRATEN-
BACH, was engraved on a brafs ring, or
plate, which encircled moft of thefe inftruments; the large ones have brafs plates
pierced, and fome with human figures
well engraved on them; thefe laft are longer
than a baffoon would be, if unfolded*;
The inhabitants fay, that it is more than a
hundred years fince thefe inftruments were
ufed, and that there is no mufician, at prefent, in the town who knows how to play on
any one of them, as they are quite different from thofe now in common ufe. In
times when commerce flourifhed in this
city, thefe inftruments ufed to be played
on every day, by a band of muficians
who attended the merchants, trading to
the Hans towns, in proceffion to the
exchange; they now hang on pegs in a
clofet, or rather prefs, with folding doors,

* The long trumpet, played lately in London,
feems only to have been an ordinary trumpet
ftraitened.

made

made on purpofe for their reception; though in the great hall there ftill lies on the floor, by them, a large fingle cafe, made of a heavy and folid dark kind of wood, fo contrived, as to be capable of receiving them all; but which, when filled with thefe inftruments, requires eight men to lift it from the ground; it was of fo uncommon a fhape, that I was unable to divine its ufe, till I was told it.

At fix o'clock this evening a fplendid proceffion paffed through the ftreets, in honour of fome legendary faint; confift-ing of a prodigious number of priefts, who fung pfalms in *canto fermo*, and fometimes in counter-point, all the way to the church, with wax tapers in their hands, accompanied by French horns, and *ferpents*; a large filver crucifix, and a *Madonna* and child, as big as the life, of the fame metal, decorated this folem-nity.

The

The Spaniards have left this good people a large portion of pride and fuperftition; the former is fhewn by the drefs and inactivity of the nobles, and the latter by the bigotry and lively faith of the reft; there are more crucifixes and virgins, in and out of the churches here, than I ever met with in any other Roman catholic town in Europe.

The proceffion above mentioned feemed to have been as much the occafion of riot and debauchery, among the common people, as the *beer* and *liberty* with which an Englifh mob is ufually intoxicated on a rejoicing night in London; there were bonfires all over the town, and the huzzas, rockets, fquibs, and crackers, were fo frequent, and fo loud, all night, in the *Place de Mer*, where I lodged, that it was impoffible to fleep; and at two o'clock in the morning the mob was fo vociferous and violent, that I thought all the inhabitants of the town had fallen together by the ears; and yet,

on

on other nights, no one of the citizens is allowed to walk in the ſtreets later than half an hour after ten, without a particular permiſſion from the governor.

This morning, at ſeven o'clock, I attended the ſinging maſter of St. Andrew's church, M. Blaviere, a Liegeois, in whoſe poſſeſſion I expected, in old manuſcript muſic, to meet with examples of the early progreſs made in counter-point by the Flamands. I found him to be very rational, intelligent, and well read in muſical authors, of which he ſhewed me ſeveral ; but there was only one among them which I had not ſeen before, and that was a treatiſe in Italian, by Franceſco Penna, Bologneſe, printed at Antwerp, in 1688. He likewiſe ſhewed me ſeveral of his own compoſitions, for the church, which convinced me that he had ſtudied hard, and was an able contra-puntiſt.

I ſpent the reſt of the morning in the Jeſuit's library, with father Newton, and father Geſquiere, who were indefatigable in ferreting out books and manuſcripts

fcripts that were likely to furnifh any
thing neceffary to my work; the latter is
one of feveral Jefuits who have been long
employed in writing the lives of the
faints, as they are placed in the Romifh
calender of each month of the year; it
is the intention of thofe authors to purge
the lives they are writing, of all the fables
which have crept into the legendary accounts of faints: upwards of fifty volumes in folio are already printed, and
more than twenty are ftill behind. The
work is written in Latin, and has for
title, *Acta Sanctorum a Johanne Bollando,
S. I. Collegi felicita cæpta a Godfredo
Henfchenio, et Daniele Pabebrochio, aucta,
digefta, & illuftrata.* Antwerpiæ, 1768.
I confulted feveral articles in the volumes
already printed, for information concerning the firft eftablifhment of chanting in
the church, its reformation by pope
Gregory the Great, with other particulars
relative to the hiftory of church mufic;
in fome of thefe I obtained more fatisfaction than other books, which I had fre-

2   quently

quently read on the fubject, had afforded
me.

The famous harpfichord makers, of the
name of Ruckers, whofe works have
been fo much, and fo long admired all
over Europe, lived in this city: there
were three, the firft, and the father
of the other two, was *John Ruckers,*
who flourifhed at the beginning of
the laft century. His inftruments were
the moft efteemed, and are remarkable
for the fweetnefs and fullnefs of their
tone. On the left hand of the found-
hole, in the bellies of thefe inftruments,
may be feen a large H, the initial of
Hans, which, in the Flemifh Language,
means John. *André,* the eldeft of John's
fons, diftinguifhed his work, by an A,
n the found-hole. His large harpfichords are lefs efteemed than thofe
made by any one of that name; but
his fmall work, fuch as fpinets, and vir-
ginals, are excellent. *Jean,* the youngeft
fon's harpfichords, though not fo good as
thofe of the father, are very much efteemed

teemed for the delicacy of their tone; his inftruments may be known by the letter I, in the found hole. The harpfi-chord-maker of the greateft eminence, after them, was J. Dan. Dulcken; he was a Heffian. At prefent there is a good workman at Antwerp, of the name of Bull, who was Dulcken's apprentice, and who fells his double harpfichords for a hun- dred ducats each, with only plain painted cafes, and without fwell or pedals; the work too of Vanden Elfche, a Flamand, has a confiderable fhare of merit; but, in general, the prefent harpfichords, made here after the Rucker model, are thin, feeble in tone, and much inferior to thofe of our beft makers in England.

I cannot quit this city, without men- tioning a particular mark of attention, with which I was honoured by father Gefquiere, the night before my departure. In the morning he had communicated to me a very ancient Latin manufcript upon mufic; but though the writing proved it

I   to

to be of great antiquity, we could not exactly fix the date of it; there were like-wife fome letters of the alphabet, ufed as mufical characters in it, which were not eafy to determine, as it was difficult to diftinguifh an A from an O, or a D, on account of the great refemblance of thefe letters in the manufcript; but by a note written in elegant Latin, with which he favoured me at night, I found that thefe difficulties had occupied his mind the whole day; indeed he feemed entirely to have fpent it in trying to clear up the firft, and offered his future fervice in re-moving the laft.

BRUSSELS.

At my return hither, from Antwerp, I employed myfelf in vifiting churches, as I had before only been at the theatre. On the day after my fecond arrival, there was a mafs, in mufic, performed in the little, but neat and elegant, church of Mary Magdalen; here are a few good

E   pictures,

pictures, with some excellent sculpture in
wood; and the portraits of the Apostles are
boldly represented in relief, or medallions,
at the sides of this church. The band of
musicians, on occasion of the festival, to
day, was but small; however, the organ
was played in a masterly manner, by M.
Straze, who is esteemed the best performer upon keyed instruments in Bruf-
sels; and several symphonies were well
executed by the whole band, during the
course of the service. Some pieces of
Italian church music were sung, not indeed so well as they would have been in
their own country; but the voices here
were far from contemptible. Two boys,
in particular, sung a duet very agreeably;
but there is generally a want of steadiness
in such young musicians, which makes
it to be wished that females were permitted in the church, to take the *soprano* part, which is generally the principal,
as the voices of females are more perma-
nent than those of boys, who are almost

always

always deprived of theirs before they
know well how to ufe them.

From this little church I went to the
cathedral of St. Gudula, where high mafs
was likewife performing, by a confiderable band of voices and inftruments. This
is the largeft church in Bruffels, the pillars are too maffive, but, upon the whole,
it is a neat and noble building; all the
beft pictures, and fome very fine tapeftry,
were expofed on occafion of this feftival,
which, on common days, cannot be feen;
it is rather loaded with tawdry ornaments, and too much begilded, as is the
cafe of moft of the Brabant churches,
which the inhabitants think they can
never make fine enough.

There is fome admirable old painting
upon glafs, in this church, with figures,
as large as the life, well preferved; thefe
paintings were by Rogiers, cotemporary
with Holbens; they were prefents from
feveral princes of thofe times, particularly John, king of Portugal, Mary, queen

of

of Hungary, Francis the firſt, of France, Ferdinand, brother to the emperor Charles the fifth, and by Charles the fifth himſelf.

The *maeſtro di capella*, who directed the band here, was M. Van Helmont. The muſic had no great effect, as the inſtruments were too few for ſo large a building; but there was a performer with a tenor voice, who ſung ſeveral Latin *motets*, compoſed by Italian maſters, reaſonably well; his voice was good, and he ſung in tune. The ſinging in the churches here is leſs French than at the theatre, as the words are always Latin, and leſs likely to corrupt the voice, and the taſte of the performer, than French words and French muſic.

In the evening I heard two muſical pieces, at the theatre, in the Flemiſh language; both were tranſlated from the French; the one was *le Tonnelier*, originally ſet to muſic by M. Duni, and the other, *Toinon et Toinetti*, ſet by M. Goſſec; the

the natives feemed highly diverted by
thefe performances, which, as dramas,
have great merit, in the original. The
mufic of meffrs. Duni and Goffec, was
preferved entire, except in a very few
places, which had been altered for the
accommodation of the Flemifh poetry, by
M. Fitzthumb.

In hearing this performance, I could
not help reflecting how eafy it was to
adapt Italian mufic to any language,
however rough and barbarous; that of
the pieces in queftion, is, for the moft
part, certainly compofed of paffages taken from Italian fongs and fymphonies,
though grafted on French words; all
the prefent compofers of French comic
operas imitate the Italian ftyle, and many
of them pillage the *buffe* operas of Italy,
without the leaft fcruple of confcience,
though they afterwards fet their names
to the plunder, and pafs it on the world
as their own property. I wifh this may
not, fometimes, be the cafe in England;
but, however that may be, it is certainly

an

an irrefragable proof of the superiority of
that melody which is become the common musical language of all Europe : not
like the French tongue, by conquest, or
policy, but received every where, by the
common consent of all who have ears sus-
ceptible of pleasure from sound, and
who give way to their own feelings.

Indeed, the French seem now the only
people in Europe, except the Italians,
who, in their dramas, have a music of
their own. The serious opera of Paris
is still in the trammels of Lulli and
Rameau, though every one who goes
thither, either yawns or laughs, except
when roused, or amused, by the dances
and decorations. As a *Spectacle*, this opera
is often superior to any other in Europe;
but, as *Music*, it is below our country psal-
mody, being without time, tune, or expression, that any but French ears can
bear : indeed the point is so much given
up, by the French themselves, that nothing but a kind of national pride, in
a few individuals, keeps the dispute alive;
the

the reft frankly confefs themfelves afhamed of their own mufic; and thofe who
defend it, muft foon give way to the
ftream of fafhion, which runs with too
much rapidity and violence to be long
ftemmed.

July 23d. Prince Charles, and the
principal perfonages of his court, were at
the play to night. The *Gageur*, a French
comedy, written by Sedaine, was admirably played, in which Mad. Verteil, an
excellent aĉtrefs, did the principal part;
after which, I heard, for the firft time,
Les deux Miliciens, a comic opera, fet by
Gretry; the mufic was worthy of that
fertile and ingenious compofer *. The
inftrumental parts were extremely well

* This author, in his fcores, is however fometimes negligent of the moft common rules of counter-point, which may proceed from writing with too
much rapidity; as it is hardly to be conceived that
a man of fuch acknowledged genius fhould have
ftudied feven or eight years, in a Confervatorio at
Naples, without acquiring a competent knowledge
of mufical grammar, and the mechanifm of his art.

exe-

executed; great effects were produced
in the ritornels, and the poetry was much
heightened by the rich and varied .co-
louring of the orcheſtra. In a muſical
drama, it frequently happens that a numerous and well diſciplined band, has
the power of imagery, of awakening
ideas, and deſcribing the paſſions, more
than a ſingle voice, or even a chorus of
many voices can attempt, with propriety ;
indeed the little opera of to-night nearly approached perfection in all its parts,
as it was well written, well ſet, well ſpoken, well acted ; and, with reſpect to the
inſtrumental parts, was well played: how
ſorry I am that truth will not allow me
to add, that it was *well ſung !*

During my reſidence at Bruſſels, I had
the pleaſure, of being made acquainted
with M. Girard, ſecretary to the literary
ſociety in this place. He is now employed,
in arranging and cataloguing the books
and manuſcripts of the Burgundy library,
which have been more than two centu-
ries

ries here ; but they have fo long remained in obfcurity and diforder, that it is not yet known, what they all contain. It was by the zeal and good offices of prince Starhemberg, that thefe books had a new room built for their reception, and that they will foon form a public library.

The manufcripts are the beft, and moft beautiful, in point of illuminations, which I ever faw : moft of them were brought to Bruffels from Burgundy, and are very ancient. It it even wonderful, to what a degree of perfection miniature painting has been carried in fome of them, particularly in one tranfcribed and illuminated at Florence, in 1485 : it was a prefent from Matthias Corvinus, king of Hungary, to the duke of Burgundy.

The arms of Burgundy are pafted in all thefe ancient manufcripts, which are divided into there claffes ; theology, hiftory and arts, poetry and romances. In the two firft, I found feveral curious and interefting particulars, relative to my work.

In

In 1745, at which time the French were in poffeffion of Bruffels; the commiffaries, and even fome of the officers, took away books and manufcripts from the Burgundy library, notwithftanding the cartel; fome of them were, indeed, returned, after the peace, upon being claimed, particularly, fuch as had been carried to the king's library, at Paris; but many others of great value, are now in the Sorbonne, and in other private hands, and cannot be recovered.

I was very politely treated by M. Girard, who attended me at the library at fix o'clock every morning, and afforded me all poffible affiftance, even to the helping me to make extracts. He likewife favoured me with a vifit at my lodgings, and gave me a letter to the elector Palatine's librarian at Manheim, and all from a very flight acquaintance, brought about by means of a note, written by M. Needham, celebrated for his micro-

microfcopic difcoveries, and his difference
with M. de Voltaire.

At Bruffels I heard a young lady play extremely well on the harp with pedals, fome
pretty pieces compofed by Godecharle,
a German, who likewife plays a good
violin, and accompanied the young lady
in thefe pieces; fhe is his fcholar: the harp
is very much played on by the ladies here,
and at Paris. It is a fweet and becom-
ing inftrument, and, by means of the
pedals for the half notes, is lefs cumbrous
and unwieldy than our double Welfh
harp. The compafs is from double Bb
to f in *altiffimo*; it is capable of great
expreffion, and of executing whatever can
be played on the harpfichord; there are
but thirty-three ftrings upon it, which,
except the laft, are the mere natural
notes of the diatonic fcale; the reft are
made by the feet *.

* This method of producing the half-tones on
the harp, by pedals, was invented at Bruffels,
about fifteen years ago, by M. Simon, who ftill
refides in that city. It is an ingenious and ufeful
con-

In attending the high mafs at the collegiate church of St. Gudula, on Sunday
26, I again heard the performance of a confiderable band of voices and inftruments;
and I was glad to find among the former
two or three women, who, though they did
not fing well, yet their being employed,
proved that female voices might have admiffion in the church, without giving offence or fcandal to piety, or even bigotry.
If the practice were to become general, of
admitting women to fing the *foprano* part
in the cathedrals, it would, in Italy, be a
fervice to mankind, and in the reft of Europe render church-mufic infinitely more
pleafing and perfect; in general, the
want of treble voices, at leaft of fuch
as have had fufficent time to be polifhed,
and rendered fteady, deftroys the effect
of the beft compofitions, in which, if

contrivance, in more refpects than one: for, by
reducing the number of ftrings, the tone of thofe
that remain, is improved; as it is well known,
that the lefs an inftrument is loaded, the more
freely it vibrates.

the

the principal melody be feeble, nothing
but the fubordinate parts, meant only
as attendants, and to enrich the harmony
of the *whole*, can be heard.

L O V A I N.

This is the laft confiderable city of
the Netherlands, in the emprefs queen's
dominions, eaft of Bruffels; it has a
univerfity, in which the youth of the
ten catholic provinces are educated,
as Leyden has for the other feven. It
was founded by John the Fourth, duke
of Brabant, in 1425; at prefent the
number of ftudents is faid to amount to
upwards of two thoufand. I remained
but a fhort time in this place, as I was
informed, that the library, which is faid
to be very rich in manufcripts, was in
fuch great diforder, that it would be difficult to find any one to my purpofe, without a longer refidence than the work which
I had allotted myfelf in Germany would
allow. I therefore contented myfelf, with

gaining

gaining what information I could, relative to the ftate of modern mufic in
that city ; and I found, that M. Kennis
is the moft remarkable performer on the
violin, in point of execution, not only
of Lovain, but of all this part of the
world. The folos he writes for his own
inftrument and hand, are fo difficult, that
no one hereabouts attempts them but
himfelf, except M. Scheppen, the *Carilloneur*, who lately, piqued by the high
reputation of M. Kennis, laid a wager,
that he would execute upon the bells
one of his moft difficult folos, to the fatisfaction of judges, appointed to determine the matter in difpute ; and he gained
not only his wager, but great honour by
his fuccefs, in fo difficult an enterprize.
This circumftance is mentioned in order
to convey fome idea to my Englifh readers, of the high cultivation of this fpecies of mufic in the Netherlands. For
there, the inhabitants of every city think
it an indifpenfible point of honour, to tell
every

every ftranger, that their *carillons* are better than all others. At Lovain, M. Van-dengheim, the organift, has the care of the chimes, and M. Scheppen plays them, by his appointment.

L I E G E.

This city has lately produced feveral good muficians, which I had met with in the Low Countries; but I found in it little worthy of remark. The organ in the cathedral is fmall, and divided into two parts, placed on each fide the choir. There is a theatre here for Flemifh plays, and fometimes for comic operas; but it was not open while I continued at Liege. The organift of the cathedral is likewife *Carilloneur*, as is often the cafe in the Netherlands; but here the paffion for chimes begins to diminifh.

M A E S T R I C K.

Here I vifited the collegiate church, belonging to the catholics, and found in it a very large organ, but it was out of tune; and the organist, M. Houghbrach, who is likewise *Carilloneur*, is no conjurer. There was a Hessian regiment, in the Dutch service, quartered in this city, which had an excellent band of music, consisting of hautbois, clarinets, *cymbala*, or *baffins*, great drum, side-drums, and triangles; and at the time of beating *la retraite*, I heard them play a considerable time on the *Place d'Armes*; at the inn too, where I lodged, I was entertained on the *dulcimer*, by a strolling boy, who seemed to have a musical genius, far superiour to his instrument and situation.

AIX LA CHAPELLE.

It was here that I first remarked the High Dutch, or German language, to be spoken by the common people, and 𝕲𝖔𝖙𝖍𝖎𝖈 letters to be used by printers.

Where the English acquired their pronunciation of *th*, I know not: it was natural to suppose that they had it from

their

their Saxon anceſtors, and to expect to
find it in Germany; but it is as much a
Shibboleth to the inhabitants of that country, as to thoſe of all the reſt of Europe.
In words where this combination of letters is uſed in orthography, it has no
other effect in pronunciation, than if the
words were written without the ʜ.
𝔚𝔢𝔯𝔱𝔥, which ſignifies worth, in Engliſh, is pronounced *wert* ; 𝔗𝔥𝔯𝔬𝔫, a
throne, *Trone* ; and 𝔗𝔥𝔢𝔬𝔩𝔬𝔤𝔲𝔰, a theo-
giſt, *Teologus.* It is no leſs difficult to
trace our peculiar ſound of the vowel I;
and as to thoſe guttural graces of pronunciation in the *ch* and *g,* of the German
language, which are ſo difficult to deſ-
cribe, and to learn, they are ſtill retained
here, and regarded as indubitable proofs
of the high antiquity of the Teutonic
dialect, though nearly loſt in her daughter the Engliſh.

As to muſic, my expectations from this
city were by no means anſwered. I
could find neither books nor muſicians

worthy

worthy of much attention. M. Kuckel-korn, organist of the famous cathedral where Charlemagne, and several succeed-ing emperors, were crowned, accompa-nies the church service very judiciously, but has no hand for extemporary playing. M. Wenzlaer has, however, a great hand on the violin; but he is a wild, half mad character, and not a deep theorist.

The passion for *carillons*, and chimes, seems here at an end; however, in the streets, through which a procession had lately passed, there were hung, to festoons and garlands, a great number of oblong pieces of glass, cut and tuned in such a manner, as to form little peals of four and five bells, all in the same key, which were played on by the wind. In walk-ing under them, I was some time un-able to discover from whence the sounds I heard proceeded; they are hung so near each other, as to be put in contact by the most gentle breeze, which may truly be called the *Carilloneur*.

J U-

J U L I E R S.

In my way through this town, to Cologn, I was entertained at the poft-houfe,
while I changed horfes, by two vaga-
bonds, who, in oppofite corners of the
room, imitated, in dialogue, all kinds of
wind inftruments, with a card and the
corner of their hats, fo exactly, that if I
had been out of their fight, I fhould not
have been able to diftinguifh the copy
from the original ; particularly in the
clarinet, French horn, and baffoon, which
were excellent. After this they *took off*
the bellowing noife of the Romifh
priefts, in chanting,, fo well, that I was
quite frightened ; for, being in a catholic town, where the inhabitants are very
zealous for the honour of their religion,
I thought it might be imagined that this
ludere facrâ, was at the inftigation of the
Englifh heretic.

CO-

C O L O G N.

I have but little to fay concerning the
mufic of this place. There was no public exhibition during the time I remained in it; however, I vifited the great
church, or cathedral, which is built upon the model of the *Duomo* at Milan, but
of common ftone; whereas, that at Milan is of white marble. There is a fimi-
larity likewife in the fate of thefe two famous churches, as both have remained
many ages unfinifhed. The plan of that
at Cologn is not above half completed;
perhaps it is owing to this, that the
choir appears much more lofty than that
at Milan. What was intended as the
approach to the choir is very low, and
arched over with bricks.

In a very fmall chapel, behind the altar,
I was fhewn the famous fhrine, in which,
it is faid, are the entire fkulls of the three
kings, who came with offerings to our
Saviour, immediately after his birth; it
has been faid that every great town has a

lion

lion to fhew to ftrangers, and this *fhrine* is the *lion* of Cologn: it is immenfely rich in gold, fculpture, jewels, antique gems, intaglios, and cameos.

The organ in this cathedral is of the moft noble and beautiful form I ever faw; its front is flat, and fpreads from pillar to pillar, over the nave of the church; it has three columns, or rather compartments, of great pipes on each fide; in the middle are three ranks of fmall pipes over each other, which form three complete and elegant buffets, and which, feparately, would be regarded as complete fronts to fmall organs; the choir organ is placed below all thefe, at the back of the player.

Mr. Weftmann is at prefent the organift. I only heard him accompany the choir in the firft fervice, which was begun when I entered the church; the fecond was chanted in *canto fermo*, without in-ftruments. It is very difficult in Roman catholic countries, to hit upon a proper time for trying an organ, or hearing an organift, as the feveral fervices continue

F 3   from

from five o'clock in the morning, till twelve at noon; and, afterwards, from two, till near night; and even during the small recefs from duty, the fervants of the church are either at dinner, or from home upon their own concerns; fo that, except during the time of divine fervice, I could hardly ever get an opportunity of hearing an organift or an organ.

In the church of St. Cecilia, I heard a nun play the organ, to the coarfe finging of her fifters; her interludes would have been thought too light for the church in England: I foon difcovered that they were not extemporary; however, they were pleafing, and well executed.

B O N N.

The elector of Cologn was not here, fo that I heard no mufic in this city; however, during winter, his highnefs has a comic opera, at his own expence, performed in his palace. Moft of his mu-ficians

ficians were now at Spa, they are all
Italians, and the *maeſtro di capella* is
Signor Lucchefe, who is a very pleaſing
compofer; when I was in Italy, I heard
Manfoli ſing a *Motet* of his compoſition,
in a church near Florence, which was
charming.

I had the honour of being very well
received by Mr. Creſſener, his majeſty's
miniſter plenipotentiary at this court,
who, not only countenanced me during
my ſhort ſtay at Bonn, but kindly furniſhed me with recommendatory letters
to feveral perfons of diſtinction in my
route.

COBLENTZ.

Italian operas are frequently performed
at this court. The elector has a good
band, in which M. Ponta, the celebrated French horn from Bohemia, whoſe
taſte and aſtoniſhing execution were
lately ſo much applauded in London, is
a performer.

F 4   The

The princefs Cunegonde, fifter to the elector of Treves, and youngeft daughter of Auguftus, king of Poland, is a very great harpfichord player. There is like- wife a moft extraordinary performer on the double bafe at this court, who plays folos on it, even worth hearing. The *maeftro di capella* of this court is Signor Sales, of Brefcia.

FRANKFORT upon the Main.

In travelling on the banks of the Rhine, from Cologne to Coblentz, I muft own, that I was aftonifhed and dif- appointed, at finding no proofs of that paffion for mufic, which the Germans are faid to poffefs, particularly along the Rhine; but even at Coblentz, though it was Sunday when I arrived there, and the ftreets and neighbourhood were crowded with people walking about for their recreation, I heard not a fingle voice or inftrument, as is ufual in moft other Roman catholic countries; I had

had therefore a mind to try another part of Germany, and croſſing the Rhine, and the terrible mountains of Wetteravia, arrived at Frankfort on the Main, much more fatigued than I was formerly after paſſing mount Cenis. Here indeed, I found a little of that diſpoſition for muſic, which I expected; and though I met no great performer vocal or inſtrumental, muſic, ſuch as it was, might be heard in all parts of the town.

The great church of St. Bartholomew, famous for being the place where the emperors are crowned, was not furniſhed with ſingers of great talents, but yet there were a number of girls, who, though the ſervice was that of the Roman catholics, were many of them Lutherans or Calviniſts, that chanted with the prieſts and canons, without the organ *.

* Though the Catholics have the great church here, yet the Lutherans are in poſſeſſion of the ſteeple, upon which they conſtantly keep a guard. A precaution, which, in peaceable times, *is ſaid to* be uſed in order to give the alarm, in caſe of fire; but, in war, they make no ſcruple to confeſs, that

§

In the ſtreets, at noon, there was likewiſe a number of young ſtudents ſinging
Hymns in three or four parts, attended
by a chaplain ; theſe are poor ſcholars
deſigned for the church, who in this manner excite the benevolence of paſſengers,
that contribute towards their cloathing.

At the inn, called the Roman Emperor,
where I lodged, after dinner there was a
band of ſtreet muſicians, who played ſeveral ſymphonies reaſonably well, in four
parts. All this happened on a day which
was not a feſtival, and therefore it is natural to believe, that the practice is common.

The organiſt of the cathedral is one of
the vicars, and much in years ; the inſtrument is not ill toned, but, like moſt
of the others which I had heard in my
route, miſerably out of tune, and the
touch ſo heavy, that the keys, like thoſe
of a *carillon*, ſeverally required the weight
of the whole hand, to put them down.

it is to watch the motions of the catholics, from
whom they are in fear of a maſſacre.

The

The labels of fome ftops in this inſtrument excited my curioſity; ſuch as the *Poſaun*, *Solicional*, *Cymbel*, *Suavial*, *Violon*, &c. in the great organ, and in the choir organ, the *Groſgeduct*, *Kleingedukt*, *Violdgamba*, &c. but, from being out of order, they were totally unfit to be played, as folo ftops. I could juſt diſcover that the *ſuavial* was meant for that ſweet ſtop in Mr. Snetzler's organs, which he calls the *Dulcian*; and the *Violon*, for the *Violona*, or double baſe; it is a half ſtop, which goes no higher than the middle C.

There *has* been a contrivance in this organ for tranſpoſing half a note, a whole note, or a flat third, higher; but it is now uſeleſs: the inſtrument was built many years ago by Meyer, and repaired, with an addition of new ſtops, fix or ſeven years ago, by Groſſwald, of Hanau. But an organ whoſe foundation is not good, is generally rendered worſe by attempts at mending it; and I remember Mr. Snetzler honeſtly telling ſome church-wardens, who aſked him, what

he

he thought an old organ, which they wanted to have repaired, was worth, and what would be the expence of mending it: he appraised it at one hundred pounds, and said, if they would lay out another hundred upon it, perhaps it would then be worth fifty.

The first instrument I heard during my stay at Frankfort, was the organ, at the Dominicans church; it was better toned, and more in tune than the rest, but it was not so good as many I have heard in England, nor was the *Vox humana* remarkably sweet, or like the human voice, though it is much admired here.

This organ has an arch cut through it, to let the light into the church from the west window; it is in a handsome case, the ornaments over the arch are in a good taste, and the side columns are well disposed. The keys are on the right hand *side* of the instrument, over which there is a small front ; the compass is

from

from C to C, the pedals have an Octave below double C.

The principal muficians in this city are, at prefent, M. Sarrazin on the violin, M. Pfeil, a gentleman performer on the harpfichord, and M. Haueifen, organift to the Calvinifts of Frankfort, at their church at Berkenheim, a little diftance from the city, in which they are not allowed a place of public worfhip.

DARMSTADT.

In paffing through this place to Manheim, I was fo fortunate, as to alight from my chaife juft as the landgrave's guards were coming on the parade. I never heard military mufic that pleafed me more; the inftruments were, four hautboys, four clarinets, fix trumpets, three on each fide the hautboys and clarinets, and thefe were flanked by two baffoons on each fide; fo that the line confifted of eighteen muficians; in the rear of thefe were cornets and clarions.

The

The whole had an admirable effect, it was extremely animating, and though trumpets and clarions are ufually too thrill and piercing, when heard in a fmall place, yet here, the parade or fquare where they mounted guard is fo fpacious that the found has room to expand in all directions, which prevents the ear from being hurt by too violent a fhock.

Before I proceed further in my mufical narrative, I muft make two or three memorandums concerning the villainous and rafcally behaviour of poftmafters and poftilions, in this part of the world ; the effects of which it is impoffible to efcape. In going over the mountains of Wetteravia, under the pretence of bad roads, *three* horfes were tied to the hurdle, called a poft-chaife, and after I had once fubmitted to this impofition, I never was allowed to ftir with lefs. At Frankfort I tried hard, but in vain, though the inn-keeper and his guefts, who were natives, all affured me, that they never had more than two horfes, when

when they travelled *extra poſt*; yet here, though no mountains were to be croſſed, the ſands were made a plea, notwith-ſtanding the roads from Frankfort to Manheim are, in every particular, the leaſt bad of any that I had yet travelled in Germany.

The women, among the common people in the country, are miſerably ugly, not, perhaps, ſo much in feature, as from dreſs, and a total neglect of complexion. They entirely hide their hair, by a kind of a ſkull-cap, uſually made of tawdry linen or cotton; they are hardly ever ſeen with ſhoes and ſtockings, though the men are furniſhed with both, ſuch as they are.

I could wiſh to ſpeak of theſe people with candour and temper, in deſpight of the bile which every ſtranger, travelling among them muſt feel at work within him; but, as I neither mean to abuſe or flatter them, I muſt ſay, that the numberleſs beggars, clamorouſly importunate, though often young, fat, ro-

6   buſt,

buft, and fit for any labour; the embar=
raffments of perpetual change and lofs
of money; the extortion, fullennefs, and
infolence of poftmafters and poftilions,
are intolerably vexatious.

M A N H E I M.

The firft mufic I heard here was mi=
litary. I lodged on the *Place d'Armes*,
or parade; the *retraite* had only drums
and fifes; and in the morning there was
nothing worth liftening to. If I had had
an inclination to defcribe, in a pompous
manner, the effects of wind inftruments
in martial mufic, there had been no
occafion to quit London; for at St.
James's, and in the Park, every morning,
we have now an excellent band; and hi=
therto, as I had not feen more foldier=
like men in any fervice than our own, fo
the mufic and muficians, of other places,
exceeded ours in nothing but the number and variety of the inftruments; our
military mufic at prefent muft feem to have
made great and hafty ftrides towards perfection,

tion, to all such as, like myself, remember, for upwards of twenty years, no other compofition made ufe of in our foot-guards, than the march in Scipio, and in our marching regiments, nothing but fide-drums.

The expence and magnificence of the court of this little city are prodigious; the palace and offices extend over almoft half the town; and one half of the inhabitants, who are in office, prey on the other, who feem to be in the utmoft indigence.

The Jefuits houfe, built by the prefent Elector, clofe to the palace, has thirty windows in front, apart from the church, which is the moft fuperb in the city; the front of the theatre, which is only a fmall wing of the palace, has likewife thirty windows.

The town itfelf is more neat, beautiful, and regular, than any which I had yet feen; its form is oval; the ftreets, like thofe of Lifle, are *tireés au cordeau,* running in ftrait lines from one

end

end to the other. There is a great
number of fquares; it contains about
1548 houfes, and in the year 1766, its
inhabitants amounted to 24190.

Thurfday, Auguft 6th. In the evening I went to the public theatre in this
town, where Zemire and Azor, tranflated
into German, and accommodated to the
pretty mufic of Mr. Gretry, was performed; it was the firft dramatic exhibition
at which I was prefent in Germany.

In fummer the Elector Palatine refides
at Schwetzingen, three leagues from
Manheim; and during that time a ftrolling
company is allowed to entertain the citizens. The performance was in a temporary booth, erected in the fquare of
the great market-place. Yet, though
nothing better than deal boards appear
without, the ftage was well decorated,
and the fcenes and dreffes were not without tafte or elegance.

I was curious to hear a German play, but
ftill more curious to hear German finging:
and

and I muſt own, that I was aſtoniſhed to find, that the German language, in ſpite of all its claſhing conſonants, and gutturals, is better calculated for muſic than the French. I am ſorry to return again to the charge; but I muſt ſay, that the great number of naſal ſounds and mute ſyllables in the French language, ſeem to corrupt and vitiate the voice, in its paſſage, more than the defect of any other language, of which I have the leaſt knowledge.

The girl who played the part of Zemire had not a great voice, but her manner of ſinging was natural and pleaſing. She had a good ſhake, and never forced her voice, or ſung out of tune; there were two of the men who had reaſonable good voices, and whoſe *portamento* and expreſſion would not have offended ſuch as had been long converſant with the beſt ſinging of Italy.

Upon the whole, I was more pleaſed with this ſinging, than with any which I had

heard

heard fince my arrival on the continent ;
indeed the Germans are now fo forward
in mufic, and have fo many excellent
compofers of their own country, that it
is matter of aftonifhment to me, that
they do not get original dramas for mufic written in their own language, and
fet by the natives: or, if they muft have
tranflations, why they do not get thofe .
tranflations new fet *.

The orcheftra here was far inferior to
that at Bruffels, in number and difcipline;
for all the great performers of this place
were now with the electŏr at Schwetzingen, fo that the fingers had no fupport
but their own merit.

Auguft 7. I fpent in the public library, which is a very fine room, with

* When I advanced farther into Germany, I
found that M. Hiller, of Leipfick, had furnifhed his
countrymen with a great number of comic operas,
in which the mufic was fo natural and pleafing,
that the favourite airs, like thofe of Dr. Arne in
England, were fung by all degrees of people ; and
the more eafy ones had the honour of being fung
in the ftreets.

fine books, but none very ancient, and few manuscripts, these being all taken away by the Bavarians in the war of 1622, and given to the Pope : they are well known in the Vatican library, by the name of the Heidelberg or Palatine Collection. The present library is said to consist of forty thousand volumes ; but though the pompous account in the *Etrennes Palatine*, speaks of manuscripts, and says, that they are kept in a chamber apart, M. Lamey, the librarian, to whom I was favoured with a letter by M. Girard, of Bruffels, confessed to me, that the collection had been too short a time in forming to be yet very rich in manuscripts, and that it contained but few of any consequence.

SCHWETZINGEN.

A list only of the performers in the service of his electoral highness, would convey a very favourable idea of the excellence of his band; it consists of near

G 3   a huna hundred hands and voices. I shall only mention here, however, some of the principal musicians employed in this orcheftra, whose names are already known in England. M. Holtzbauer, is one of the chapel masters. M. Christian Canabich, and Charles Toeschi, are the principal violins; the former leads in the Italian operas, and the latter in the French and German. These three masters are authors of several excellent *symphonies*, some of which have been printed in England. M. J. Baptist Wendling, is the principal flute here, and among the violins are John Toeschi, Frenzel, Fr. and Charles Wendling, and Kramer. This last is reckoned one of the best solo players in Europe; however, I shall say but little about him here, as he is now in England, and my countrymen have an opportunity of judging of his talents for themselves. There are twenty-three vocal performers in this band, several of which deserve to be distinguished, particularly

cularly Mademoifelle Wendling, Mademoifelle Danzy, and Madame Kramer. Signori Roncaglio, Pefarini, and Saporofi.

Many of the performers on the court lift, are either fuperannuated or fupernumeraries; but of the former, after having ferved the elector for a number of years, if by ficknefs or accident they happen to lofe their voice or talents, they have a handfome penfion, which they enjoy as long as they live at Manheim; and even if they chufe to retire into their own country, or elfewhere, they are ftill allowed half their penfion.

I wanted very much to come to my principal point of hearing the beft of thefe performers; but nothing can be done precipitately in Germany. *Feftine lente* feems here a favourite motto. It was neceffary to vifit, the firft day, and to be vifited the fecond; and, on the third, there was fome chance, but no certainty, of obtaining the favour I required.

It

It has frequently been said, that bluntness, and a thorough contempt of every person and thing, which is not entirely English, mark my honest countryman, *John Bull*, in every part of the world. I am unwilling to indulge national reflections; however, now and then a *single* character certainly appears, which calls to mind, all that has been said of a *whole* people. The French Abbé I met with at Antwerp, was what many would have called a *true Frenchman* ; and I met with several afterwards, who would be called *true Germans*, for slow apprehension and inactivity. If, in the morning, I had explained as clearly as I could, the object of my journey, and shewn the general plan of my future work, to a man of letters, a librarian, or a musician, it was common for that individual, in the evening, to say " the History of Music, I think " you are going to write—hum—ay, " the History of Music — hum —well, " and what do you wish I should do for you ?"

" you ?" Here I was forced, in a painful *Da Capo*, to tell my ftory over again, and to beg his affiftance.

Travelling is not very common in this country; and people here, like the Engliſh, are ſhy of ſtrangers, and wiſhing to ſhake them off. In France, and Italy, the inhabitants are uſed to do the honours, and do them well. As to my particular enquiries here, which, in fact, concerned their honour more than my own, I gained but little affiftance; it was difficult to difcover who *could* afford me any, and much more to find thoſe that *would*. I fometimes wiſhed to employ the town cryer, at my firſt entrance into a German city, to tell the muſical inhabitants who I was, and what I wanted; for it frequently happened, where his majeſty had no miniſter, that I was on the point of quitting a place before this was known.

Sunday, 9th Auguſt. This evening I was at the repreſentation of *La Contadi-*

na

na in Corte, a comic opera, at the Elector's theatre, adjoining to his palace. The music was composed by Signor Sacchini, and was full of that clearness, grace, and elegant simplicity, which characterise the productions of that author. The vocal parts were performed by Signor Giorgietto, an Italian *soprano,* whose voice was but feeble, nor were his abilities very considerable in other particulars. Signora Francesca Danzi, a German girl, whose voice and execution are brilliant; she has likewise a pretty figure, a good shake, and an expression as truly Italian, as if she had lived her whole life in Italy; in short, she is now a very engaging and agreeable performer, and promises still greater things in future, being young, and having never appeared on any stage till this summer. Signor Zonca, an Italian tenor, who was in England some years ago; his highest praise is, that he does not offend; and Signora Allegrante, a young Italian, under the care of M.

Holtz-

Holtzbaur, fings in a pretty unaffected manner; and though her voice will not allow her to afpire at the firft part in an opera, fhe feems likely to fill the fecond in a very engaging manner. There were two dances between the acts, one of which, reprefenting a German fair, was the moft entertaining I ever faw; one of the principal dancers here is the daughter of the late celebrated Stamitz, from whofe fire and genius the prefent ftyle of *Sinfonies*, fo full of great effects, of light and fhade, may in a confiderable degree be derived.

The Elector, Electrefs, and princefs royal of Saxony, were prefent at this performance. The theatre, though fmall, is convenient; the decorations and dreffes ingenious and elegant, and there was a greater number of attendants and figurers than ever I faw in the great opera, either of Paris or London: in the dance, reprefenting a German fair, there were upwards of a hundred perfons on the ftage

at

at one time ; but this opera is very in-
confiderable, compared with that at
Manheim, in the winter, which is performed in one of the largeft and moft
fplendid theatres of Europe, capable of
containing five thoufand perfons ; this
opera begins the fourth of November,
and continues generally, twice a week, till
Shrove-Tuefday.

I was informed that the mere illuminations of the Manheim theatre, with wax
lights, coft the elector upwards of forty
pounds, at each reprefentation ; and that
the whole expence of bringing a new
opera on this ftage, amounted to near
four thoufand pounds. The great theatre,
the enfuing winter, was to be opened
with an opera compofed by Mr. J. Bach,
who was daily expected here from London, when I was at Manheim.

I cannot quit this article, without doing juftice to the orcheftra of his electoral highnefs, fo defervedly celebrated
throughout Europe. I found it to be
indeed

indeed all that its fame had made me expect : power will naturally arife from a great number of hands; but the judicious ufe of this power, on all occafions, muft be the confequence of good difcipline; indeed there are more folo players, and good compofers in this, than perhaps in any other orcheftra in Europe; it is an army of generals, equally fit to plan a battle, as to fight it.

But it has not been merely at the Elector's great opera that inftrumental mufic has been fo much cultivated and refined, but at his *concerts*, where this extraordinary band has " ample room and verge enough," to difplay all its powers, and to produce great effects without the impropriety of deftroying the greater and more delicate beauties, peculiar to vocal mufic ; it was here that Stamitz firft furpaffed the bounds of common opera overtures, which had hitherto only ferved in the theatre as a kind of court cryer, with an " O Yes !" in order to awaken attention, and befpeak filence,

silence, at the entrance of the singers.
Since the discovery which the genius
of Stamitz first made, every effect has
been tried which such an aggregate of
sound can produce ; it was here that the
Crescendo and *Diminuendo* had birth ; and
the *Piano*, which was before chiefly
used as an echo, with which it was generally synonimous, as well as the *Forte*,
were found to be musical *colours* which
had their *shades*, as much as red or blue
in painting.

I found, however, an imperfection in
this band, common to all others, that I
have ever yet heard, but which I was in
hopes would be removed by men so attentive and so able ; the defect, I mean,
is the want of truth in the wind instruments. I know it is natural to those
instruments to be out of tune, but some
of that art and diligence which these great
performers have manifested in vanquish-
ing difficulties of other kinds, would
surely be well employed in correcting
this

this leaven, which fo much fours and cor-
rupts all harmony. This was too plainly
the cafe to-night, with the baffoons and
hautbois, which were rather too fharp,
at the beginning, and continued grow-
ing fharper to the end of the opera.

My ears were unable to difcover any other
imperfection in the orcheftra, throughout
the whole performance; and this imperfection is fo common to orcheftras, in general,
that the cenfure will not be very fevere
upon this, or afford much matter for triumph to the performers of any other orcheftra in Europe.

The Elector, who is himfelf a very
good performer on the German flute,
and who can, occafionally, play his part
upon the violoncello, has a concert in his
palace every evening, when there is no
public exhibition at his theatre; but
when that happens, not only his own
fubjects, but all foreigners have admiffion
gratis.

The

The going out from the opera at
Schwetzingen, during fummer, into
the electoral gardens, which, in the
French ftyle, are extremely beautiful,
affords one of the gayeft and moft
fplendid fights imaginable; the country
here is flat, and naked, and therefore
would be lefs favourable to the free and
open manner of laying out grounds in
Englifh horticulture, than to that which
has been adopted. The orangery is
larger than that at Verfailles, and perhaps than any other in Europe.

His electoral highnefs's fuite at Schwetzingen, during fummer, amounts to fifteen
hundred perfons, who are all lodged in
this little village, at his expence.

To any one walking through the ftreets
of Schwetzingen, during fummer, this
place muft feem to be inhabited only by
a colony of muficians, who are conftantly exercifing their profeffion: at one
houfe a fine player on the violin is heard;

at

at another, a German flute; here an excellent hautbois; there a baffoon, a clarinet,
a violoncello, or a concert of feveral inftruments together. Mufic feems to be
the chief and moft conftant of his Electoral highnefs's amufements; and the
operas, and concerts, to which all his
fubjects have admiffion, forms the judgment, and eftablifhes a tafte for mufic,
throughout the electorate.

LUDWIGSBURG.

It is no uncommon thing, in Germany, for a fovereign prince, upon a
difference with his fubjects, to abandon
the ancient capital of his dominions, and
to erect another at a fmall diftance from
it, which, in procefs of time, not only
ruins the trade, but greatly diminifhes
the number of its inhabitants, by attract-
ing them to his new refidence: among
the princes who come under this predi-
cament, are the elector of Cologn, removed to *Bonn*; the Elector Palatine,

H   removed

removed from Heidelberg, to *Manheim*; and the duke of Würtemberg, from Stutgard to *Ludwigſburg*.

The ground upon which this town is built, is irregular and wild, yet it contains many fine ſtreets, walks, and houſes. The country about it is not pleaſant, but very fertile, eſpecially in vines, producing a great quantity of what is called Neckar wine.

Though Stutgard is nominally the capital of the dutchy of Würtemburg, it has not, for ten years paſt, been the reſidence of its ſovereign; and though the operas, and muſical eſtabliſhments of this prince, uſed, during the ſeven years direction of Jomelli, to be the beſt and moſt ſplendid in Germany, they are now but the ſhadow of what they were: indeed the expence ſo far exceeded the abilities of his ſubjects to ſupport, that the Germans ſay the duke of Würtemberg's paſſion for muſic was carried to ſuch exceſs as to ruin both his country and people, and to

8   oblige

oblige his fubjects to remonftrate againft his prodigality at the diet of the empire.

At prefent his highnefs feems œconomifing, having reformed his operas and orcheftra, and reduced a great number of old performers to *half* pay : but, as moft muficians have too great fouls to live upon their *whole* pay, be it what it will, this reduction of their penfions is regarded, by the principal of thofe in the fervice of this court, as a difmiffion; fo that thofe who have vendible talents, demand permiffion to retire, as faft as opportunities offer, for engaging themfelves elfewhere.

The German courts are fo much dazzled by their own fplendor, as to be wholly blind to what is doing at the diftance only of a day's journey among their neighbours; hence, I never found, in any of them, exactly what report had made me expect. Upon quitting Schwetzingen, I deviated fomewhat from the direct

H 2   road

road to Vienna, in order to vifit Ludwigfburg, at which place I was told I fhould
not only find the duke of Würtemburg,
but likewife hear fine operas, concerts,
and great performers; but, alas! after
being roafted alive, and jumbled to death,
in a *wagon*, which the Germans call a
poft-chaife, for fourteen or fifteen hours,
while I travelled feventy - five miles;
when I came to Ludwigfburg, I found the
information which I had received fo far
from exact, that the duke of Wurtemburg
was at Gravenic, thirteen leagues off, and
fcarce a mufician of eminence left in the
town. However I obtained an exact ftate
of the prefent mufical eftablifhment of
the Wirtemburg court, ftage, and church.

The firft *macftro di capella*, is Signor
Boroni. The *foprano* voices are, Signora
Bonani, and Seeman, Signor Muzio, and
Signor Gurreieri, *Caftrati* ; *Contralti*,
Rubinelli, and Paganelli. Among the
tenors, the duke had laft winter a great
lofs by the death of the admirable Cav.
Ettori,

Ettori, who was reckoned, by the Italians, the best singer of his kind on the serious opera stage: there are eighteen violins, with Signor Lolli at their head, among the rest, are Curz, and Baglioni; this last is a very good player, and of the famous Bolognia family; there are six tenors, three violoncellos, and four double bases; the principal organists are, Frederick Seeman, and Schubart; four hautbois, Alrich, Hitsch, Blesner, and Commeret; flutes, Steinhardt, a very good one, and Augustinelli; three horns; two bassoons, Schwartz, an admirable one, and Bart.

For the *Opera Buffa*, Signore Bonani, Seeman, Liberati, Frigeri: Signori Messieri, Rossi, Cosimi, Liberati, and Righetti.

Dancers, male and female, thirty-two; principals, Balliby, Franchi, and Riva. Upwards of ninety persons are on the pension list for these operas; but many are kept in it long after they become unfit for service; and it is likewise swelled

with

with the names of perfons of no great importance, fuch as inftrument carriers, copyifts, and bellows-blowers.

. This prince had two new ferious operas laft winter, the one compofed by Jomelli, and the other by Sacchini. The theatre is immenfe, and is open at the back of the ftage, where there is an amphitheatre, in the open air, which is fometimes filled with people, to produce effects in perfpective; it is built, as are all the theatres which I had yet feen in Germany, upon the Italian model.

The duke of Würtemburg, who is fo expenfive in the mufic of his court and theatre, has no other inftruments among his troops, that I heard, than trumpets, drums, and fifes. The moft fhining parts of a German court, are ufually its *military*, its *mufic*, and its *hunt*. In this laft article the expence is generally enormous; immenfe forefts and parks, fet apart for a prince's amufement, at the expence of agriculture, commerce, and, indeed,

indeed, the neceffaries of life, keep vaft tracts of land uncultivated, and his fubjects in beggary.

The foldiery of this prince's prefent capital are fo numerous, confifting never of lefs than fix thoufand in time of peace, that nothing like a gentleman can be feen in the ftreets, except officers. The foldiers feem difciplined into clock-work. I never faw fuch mechanical exactnefs in animated beings. One would fuppofe that the author of " *Man a Machine,*" had taken his idea from thefe men: their appearance, however, is very formidable; black whifkers, white peruques, with curls at the fides, fix deep; blue coats, patched and mended with great ingenuity and diligence. There are two fpacious courts, one before, and one within the palace, full of military.

This prince, who is himfelf a good player on the harpfichord, had, at one time, in his fervice, three of the greateft performers on the violin in Europe, Fe-

H 4   rari,

rari, Nardini, and Lolli; on the hautbois, the two Plas, a famous baffoon,
Schwartz, who is ftill here; and Walther,
on the French horn; with Jomelli to
compofe; and the beft ferious and comic
fingers of Italy. At prefent, indeed, his
lift of muficians is not fo fplendid; however, his œconomy is, I believe, more in
appearance than reality; for at *Solitude,*
a favourite fummer palace, he has, at an
enormous expence, eftablifhed a fchool of
arts, or Confervatorio, for the education
of two hundred poor and deferted children of talents; of thefe a great number
are taught mufic, and from thefe he has
already drawn feveral excellent vocal and
inftrumental performers, for his theatre:
fome are taught the learned languages,
and cultivate poetry; others, acting and
dancing. Among the fingers, there are
at prefent fifteen Caftrati, the court having in its fervice two Bologna furgeons,
expert in this vocal manufacture. At Ludwigfburg there is likewife a Confervatorio

torio for a hundred girls, who are educated in the fame manner, and for the
fame purpofes ; the building conftructed
at *Solitude,* for the reception of the boys,
has a front of fix or feven hundred feet.

It is the favourite amufement of the
duke of Wurtemburg to vifit this fchool;
to fee the children dine, and take their
leffons. His paffion for mufic and fhews,
feems as ftrong as that of the emperor
Nero was formerly. It is, perhaps, upon
fuch occafions as thefe, that mufic becomes a vice, and hurtful to fociety;
for that nation, of which half the fubjects are ftage-players, fidlers, and foldiers, and the other half beggars, feems
to be but ill governed. Here nothing is
talked of but the adventures of actors,
dancers, and muficians.—In this article
I have perhaps gone beyond my *laft.*

I can proceed no further in my account of this place, without making
my acknowledgements to M. Schubart,
organift of the Lutheran church : he
was the firft real great harpfichord player
that

that I had hitherto met with in Germany, as well as the first who seemed to think the object of my journey was, in some measure, a national concern. I travelled not as a musician usually travels, to *get* money, but to *spend* it, in search of musical merit and talents, wherever I could find them, in order to display them to my countrymen. M. Schubart seemed sensible of this, and took all possible pains to please my ears, as well as to satisfy my mind. He is formed on the Bach school; but is an enthusiast, and original in genius. Many of his pieces are printed in Holland; they are full of taste and fire. He played on the Clavichord, with great delicacy and expression; his finger is brilliant, and fancy rich; he is in possession of a perfect double shake, which is obtained but by few harpsichord players.

He was some time organist of Ulm, where he had a fine instrument to play on; but here he has a most wretched one.
His

His merit is but little known where he is at prefent planted : the common peo-ple think him mad, and the reft overlook him.

. We communicated our thoughts to each other in a fingular manner : I was not, as yet, able to keep pace with his ideas, or my own impatience to know them, in German; and he could nei-ther fpeak French nor Italian, but could converfe in Latin very fluently, having been originally intended for the church; and it amazed me to find, with what quicknefs and facility he expreffed what-ever he would, in Latin ; it was literally, a living language in his hands. I gave him the plan of my Hiftory of Mufic to read, in German; and, to convince me, that he clearly underftood my meaning, he tranflated it, that is, read it aloud to me in Latin, at firft fight. My pronuncia-tion of Latin, if I had been accuftomed to fpeak it, would not have been intelli-gible to him; but as he underftood Ita-lian,

lian, though he could not speak it, our conversation was carried on in two different languages, Latin and Italian; so that the questions that were asked in one of these tongues, were answered in the other. In this manner we kept on a loquacious intercourse the whole day, during which, he not only played a great deal on the Harpsichord, Organ, Piano forte, and Clavichord; but shewed me the theatre, and all the curiosities of Ludwigsburg, as well as wrote down for me, a character of all the musicians of that court and city.

And, in the evening, he had the attention to collect together, at his house, three or four boors, in order to let me hear them play and sing *national music*, concerning which, I had expressed great curiosity.

The public library here has not been formed many years, and is as yet not very rich in manuscripts, or ancient books; the history professor and librarian

6   M.

M. Urot, a native of France, was very polite, and took great pains to fatisfy my curiofity, particularly, in fhewing me a very extraordinary aftronomical machine or orrery, which M. Hahn, minifter at Onftmettingen, in the bailiwic of Balingen, invented and executed, in the fpace of eighteen months, and which his ferene highnefs the duke of Würtemburg has purchafed for the public library.

It is compofed of three parts, that are put in motion by the weights of a common clock, which is wound up every eight days, and whofe *pendulum* vibrates feconds.

In the middle part are three dials, placed perpendicularly.

The upper one fimply marks hours, and minutes.

The next, in which are fixed the figns of the zodiac, indicates the hours of the day, the days of the week, and the days of the month, without its ever being

being neceffary to regulate the index, for
the unequal number of days in different
months.

And the laft dial, upon the great circle, on which are diftinguifhed, the cen-
turies of 8000 years, has two principal
indices, one of which points out the
prefent century, and the other, the prefent year.

Of the two collateral parts of this
machine, that on the right hand repre-
fents the Copernican fyftem ; and that on
the left, the apparent courfe of the heavenly bodies. Thefe parts are put in
motion, by the principal fpring of the
clock in the middle, and correfpond fo
perfectly, that no variation in their
movements, or in the different afpects of
the heavenly bodies has ever been difcovered ; and both have been found conftantly conformable to the calculations
of the moft exact ephemeris.

This whole machine is fo conftructed,
that without any rifk of putting it out of
order,

order, or fpoiling it, the reciprocal pofi-
tions of the planets and conftellations,
fuch as they *will* be in any future minute, or fuch as they *have* been, in any
one that is paft, may be feen; fo that
this machine takes in all time; the paft,
prefent, and future ; and is, not only an
orrery for thefe times, but a perpetual,
accurate, and minute hiftory of the hea-
vens for all ages.

The defcription of this piece of mechanifm, by profeffor Vifcher, librarian
of the public library, taken from the
writings, and experiments, of the inventor,
M. Hahn, will give the public a more
perfect idea than I am able to do of this
amazing machine, which in Germany,
is greatly admired by the learned in
aftronomy and mechanics *.

---

* This defcription was publifhed at Stutgard,
in the German language, in 1770. It contains
twenty-eight pages, in quarto, and has for title,
Befchreibung einer Aftronomifchen Mafchine,
welche fich in der öffentlichen Herzoglichen Bibli-
othek zu Ludwigsburg befindet.

U L M.

U L M.

I cannot fay much for the beauty of this old city; however, its cathedral is one of the largeſt, higheſt, and beſt preſerved Gothic buildings I have ſeen. Its organ is ſo much celebrated by travellers, for ſize and goodneſs, that it excited in me a great deſire to ſee and examine it; but I was ſomewhat diſappointed in finding it neither ſo ancient, ſo large, or ſo full of ſtops as I expected. It was built but thirty-eight years ago; the builder, M. Schmahl, is ſtill living, and he and his ſon, who were cleaning it, were ſo obliging as to furniſh me with an account of its contents.

The Gallery, and ornaments of this inſtrument, are a hundred and fifty feet high; it contains forty-five ſtops, three ſets of keys, and pedals; the largeſt pipes are ſixteen feet long, and the ſum total of pipes amounts to 3442.

The German flute in this organ ſeems the beſt of the ſolo ſtops, the reed-work is pretty good, but there is no ſwell.

The prefent organift is not reckoned a great player; and I could not find, upon enquiry, that this city is now in poffef-fion of one capital performer upon any inftrument.

Ulm ufed to be famous for its company of 𝔐innefänger𝔰, or *Laudifti*, like that at Florence; but it now no longer fubfifts.

My neareft and cheapeft way, from hence to Vienna, would have been down the Danube, which is a paffage of 600 miles by water; but I could not refift the defire of feeing Augfburg and Mu-nich, or indeed reconcile to myfelf the neglect of thofe two cities, which had fo fair a claim to my notice among the principal places in Germany. I there-fore determined to crofs, not defcend, the Danube, in order to vifit

AUGSBURG.

I arrived here on Saturday morning, the 15th July, about feven o'clock, after

I

tra-

travelling all night, and luckily went to
the cathedral between eight and nine,
where I heard part of a German sermon,
and a mass, in music, performed by two
choirs * ; being a festival, the church
was very much crowded. It is a small
and ordinary building, but richly and
tawdrily ornamented ; there are, however, two large and elegant organs, one
on each side the west end of the choir.
One of these was well played, but in a
way more masterly than pleasing ; the
rage for crude, equivocal, and affected
modulation, which now prevails generally all over Germany, renders voluntary
playing so unnatural, that it is a perpetual disappointment and torture to the
ear ; which is never to expect any thing
that comes, or to have one discord resolv-
ed, but by another. A little of this high

* This church is in the possession of the Catholics, one half of the inhabitants of this free
city are Protestants, who have not only churches
allowed them, but also an equal share in the go-
vernment,

sauce,

fauce, difcreetly ufed, produces great
and furprifing effects; but, for ever to
be feeking for far-fetched and extraneous
harmony, is giving a man that is hungry, nothing but *Chian* to eat, inftead
of plain and wholefome food.

The mufic of the mafs was in a good
ftyle; there was an agreeable mixture of
ancient and modern, and fome of the vocal parts were pleafingly performed;
particularly by two boys and a tenor,
whofe voices were good, and who had feveral folo verfes and duets given them;
and from what I heard this day, I was
confirmed in my opinion, that, except
the Italian, the German manner of finging
is lefs vicious and vulgar, than that of any
other people in Europe. There was a
folo concerto introduced on the violin,
which, though difficult, was neatly executed. The reft of the violins were weak
and ordinary.

There was a rude and barbarous flourifh
of drums and trumpets at the elevation

of

óf the Hoft, which was what I had never heard before, except at Antwerp.

Having been told, that M. Seyfurth, the cantor, a celebrated finger, and fcholar of M. C. P. E. Bach, to whom I had letters, was out of town, I ftayed but a fhort time at Augfburg; for, to fay the truth, I was fomewhat tired of going to imperial cities after mufic; as I feldom found any thing but the organ and organift worth attending to, and not always them; for they, like thofe in our country towns, are fometimes good, and fometimes bad. Thefe cities are not rich, and therefore have not the folly to fupport their theatres at a great expence. The fine arts are children of affluence and luxury: in defpotic governments they render power lefs infupportable, and diverfion from thought is perhaps as neceffary as from action. Whoever therefore feeks mufic in Germany, fhould do it at the feveral courts, not in the free imperial cities, which are generally inhabited

habited by poor induſtrious people, whoſe
genius is chilled and repreſſed by penury;
who can beſtow nothing on vain pomp or
luxury; but think themſelves happy, in
the poſſeſſion of neceſſaries. The reſidence of a ſovereign prince, on the contrary, beſides the muſicians in ordinary of the
court, church, and ſtage, ſwarms with
penſioners and expectants, who have however few opportunities of being heard.

Augſburg is a very large and fine old
city; ſome of the houſes are whimſically
pretty, from the manner in which they
are plaiſtered and ornamented, and a
few of the ſtreets are rather wide; but
the generality of the houſes have their
gable ends in front, as in the Netherlands. The town-houſe, with ſome of
the ſpires are well worth ſeeing; and at
going out on the Munich ſide, there is a
very fine building, juſt conſtructed, for
the uſe of a cotton manufactory, which
is of an immenſe ſize, and in a pleaſing
ſtyle of architecture.

The

The head drefs of the women here is very fingular; they wear a kind of gold fkull-cap; fome a broad border of gold lace, and the reft filled up by work in different colours, but moftly all gold embroidery; and here, as well as throughout Bavaria, the Roman catholic women conftantly walk the ftreets with a rofary in their hands, which is a fafhion and ornament here as much as an implement of devotion.

I was much diftreffed during my fhort ftay in this city, by the following adven-venture. I had fent my fervant, and, at prefent, my interpreter, Pierre, a Lie-geois, that I had brought with me from Antwerp, to enquire out, while the mafs was performing, the habitation of M. Seyfurth, to whom I had been recom-mended by a friend at Hamburg. I had defired him to return to the church when he had executed his commiffion, in order to conduct me back to my inn. I waited pati-ently till ten o'clock, when all the mufic was over, but no Pierre! I walked about the

church,

church, till I was tired, and afhamed to
ftay any longer, but no Pierre! I walked
round the church, and up and down the
ftreets in fight of it, for I durft venture no
farther, not knowing even the *name* of my
inn; and I had, indeed, very little language
in which to explain my fituation to thefe
cold, and, in appearance, furly people.
What could I do, but return to the
church and walk about again? this I did
till paft two o'clock, when I feared being
fufpected as a ftranger, of a defign to rob
the church of fome of its treafures; but
no Pierre! at length I was compelled to
take courage, and try to make my circumftances, known: I perufed every idle
countenance to difcover good nature in it.
I accofted feveral in vain, till an old beg-
gar-man applied to me for relief; I gave
him two or three *ireuzers*, and thought
that " one good turn deferved another."
I recollected the having been fet down
by the poft-wagon, on my arrival, at a
poft-houfe: there are feveral in large German cities. Welches ist der Weg nach dem

Pof=

𝔓𝔬𝔰𝔱𝔥𝔞𝔲𝔰 𝔤𝔲𝔱𝔢𝔯 𝔉𝔯𝔢𝔲𝔫𝔡 ? here was a gib-
ble-gabble, which ended with, 𝔡𝔦𝔢 𝔅𝔯𝔦𝔢𝔣𝔢 ?
meaning, was it the poſt-houſe for letters ? 𝔑𝔢𝔦𝔫, ſaid I, 𝔡𝔢𝔯 𝔓𝔬𝔰𝔱𝔴𝔞𝔤𝔢𝔫 𝔫𝔞𝔠𝔥
𝔘𝔩𝔪 𝔤𝔢𝔥𝔢𝔱 𝔥𝔦𝔢𝔯𝔞𝔟 — 𝔍𝔞, 𝔧𝔞, 𝔦𝔠𝔥 𝔳𝔢𝔯𝔰𝔱𝔢𝔥𝔢
𝔰𝔦𝔢. At length we found this houſe ; but
then I knew not either what to ſay or do.
I blundered out as well as I could, that
I wanted the 𝔥𝔞𝔲𝔰 where my baggage had
been carried in the morning.　But could
not recollect the word 𝔚𝔦𝔯𝔱𝔥𝔰, an inn ;
it turned out to be the Lamb, 𝔡𝔞𝔰 𝔏𝔞𝔪𝔪,
and when I found it, my joy was as
great as that of a good chriſtian pilgrim
would have been in a Pagan country, at
the ſight of an *Agnus Dei*. Where ſhould
the faithful Pierre, my honeſt Liegeois,
have been all this while, but on his bed,
comfortably and faſt aſleep ? and I did
not diſcover, till two months after, that
he had never ſought Mr. Seyfurth, to
whom I had ſent him, but had deemed
it eaſier to find a bed, and to make me
believe he was out of town, than to wear
out his ſhoes in ſtrolling about a ſtrange
place,

place, after a perfon, with whom he had
no bufinefs which concerned himfelf. But,
in order to make the difappointment fomewhat more palatable to me, he faid, that
the gentleman was only gone to Munich, for a few days, and that I fhould
certainly find him there.

M U N I C H.

I was amply rewarded for the trouble
I took in vifiting this city, as I not only
found in it materials of great importance
to my Hiftory, but a great number of modern muficians of the firft clafs, whofe
performance and converfation were delightful and inftructive. I had likewife
the honour of being well received, and
even affifted in my enquiries, by perfons
of all ranks; a happinefs for which I am
greatly indebted to the friendly and active
zeal of our minifter at this court, M. de
Vifme, whofe learning, knowledge, and
experience, joined to a fteady benevolence and hofpitality, all confpired to
render

render my refidence at Munich both profitable and pleafant.

I arrived here on Sunday morning, the
16th Auguft. The firft thing I did was
to wait on M. de Vifme, with my cre-
dentials, that is, my recommendatory letters; which having read, and received a
more particular information of the object
of my journey from myfelf, he fent immediately to Signor Don Panzachi, an
excellent tenor finger, of the Elector of
Bavaria's ferious opera, who having refided feveral years in this city, was well
qualified to inform me of fuch perfons
as were beft worth hearing and converfing with; and he gave every day, during my refidence here, proofs of his zeal
and intelligence. I was likewife indebted
to this gentleman for a very particular account of the mufic of Spain, where he had
refided nine years; and he was not only fo
kind as to lend me many curious Spanifh
books, on the fubject of mufic, but to fing to
me feveral *Tonadillas* and *Seguidillas*, which
he

he is faid, by perfons who have been in
Spain, to do as well, that is, as truly, as
is poffible for one not a native of that
country.

I was fo fortunate as to find here,
Signor Guadagni, and Signora Mingotti,
who both rendered me very fingular fervices, in the moft polite and agreeable manner; and I was the more flattered and
pleafed by their attention, as they are
performers of fuch high rank, who have
feen fo much fervice, and by whofe great
abilities, in their profeffion, I have been
fo frequently delighted in England.
They both profefs the higheft refpect,
gratitude, and reverence for individuals
in England, but make great complaints
againft the public, with what reafon I
fhall not pretend to determine, as it is
not my intention to fight the battles o'er
again, of two fuch able champions: I
own myfelf fo partial to talents, where-
ever I find them, that when they are attacked, I conftantly incline to their fide.
Gua-

[124]

Guadagni complains of illiberal treatment from the public, who, when he sung in the opera of Orfeo, merely to oblige them, and Sir W. W. without fee or reward, hissed him for going off the stage, when he was encored, with no other design than *to return in character*.

Signora Mingotti says too, that she was frequently hissed in England, for having the tooth-ach, a cold, or a fever, to which the good people of England will readily allow every human being is liable, except an actor or a singer. I know that the public are infidels in these matters, and with reason, as their hearts are hardened by repeated imposition; but, however, notwithstanding the many *pseudo* colds and fevers among theatrical performers, it is just possible for these people to have *real* disorders, otherwise they would bid fair for immortality.

Signor Guadagni came to Munich from Verona, with the Electress dowager of
Saxony,

Saxony, fifter to this Elector, and daughter of the emperor Charles the feventh.
This princefs is celebrated all over Europe for her talents, and the progrefs fhe
has made in the arts, of which fhe is a
conftant protectrefs.

Her highnefs is a poetefs, a paintrefs,
and fo able a mufician, that fhe plays,
fings, and compofes, in a manner which
Dilettanti feldom arrive at. She has,
among other things, written in Italian, two operas, which fhe has herfelf
fet to mufic, *Taleftri*, and *il Trionfo della
Fedeltà*; both are printed in Score, at Leipfic, and are much admired all over Germany, where they have frequently been
performed. This is bringing about a re-
conciliation between mufic and poetry,
which have fo long been at variance, and
feparated. Among the ancients, the poet
and mufician were conftantly united in
the fame perfon; but modern times have
few examples of fuch a junction, except
in this princefs, and in M. Rouffeau, who
was

was not only author of the poetry, but of the mufic of his little drama, the *Devin du Village*.

Signora Mingotti has not, as I could find, any penſion from this court; but ſhe has friends, to whom ſhe is attached, and ſays that ſhe can live much cheaper here than in England, otherwiſe ſhe ſhould have ſpent her ſmall income, and the remainder of her days, there.

The firſt ſinger in the ſerious opera here, is Signor Rauzzini, a young Roman performer, of ſingular merit, who has been ſix years in the ſervice of this court; but is engaged to ſing in an opera compoſed by young Mozart, at the next carnival at Milan; he is not only a charming ſinger, a pleaſing figure, and a good actor; but a more excellent contrapuntiſt, and performer on the harpſichord, than a ſinger is uſually allowed to be, as all kind of application to the harpſichord, or compoſition, is ſuppoſed, by the Italians, to be prejudicial to the voice. Signor Rauzzini

ni has set two or three comic operas here, which have been very much approved; and he shewed and sung to me several airs of a serious cast, that were well written, and in an exquisite taste.

The day after my arrival, I had the pleasure of dining with Guadagni, Rauzzini, and Ravanni, an Italian counter-tenor, in the service of this court, and after dinner of hearing them sing trios most divinely.

At night I went with them to the comic opera, at the little theatre; at which were the Elector, the Electress, the Electress dowager of Saxony, the Margrave of Baden, and the Duchess of Bavaria; the piece was called *l'Amore senza Malizia*, and was set by Signor Ottane, of Bologna, a scholar of Padre Martini, mentioned in my Italian musical journey. Signora Lodi, who performed the principal woman's part, pleased me much, by the clearness and brilliancy of her voice, as well as by her elegant manner of sing-

8   ing

ing and acting; if there is any defect in her voice, it is that sometimes it meets with a little obstruction in the throat; and one would wish that she had, as to person, a little less *embonpoint*. There was a tenor in this opera, a German, M. Adamont, whose voice and manner of singing were very pleasing; and a Baritono, Signor Guglielmini, a man whose action and humour make some amends for a total want of voice. After the opera, I supped with the same company which I had dined with, and was again delighted with trios, sung in such a way, as one never can hope to hear in public, and the chances are many against it in private.

The library of the Elector is more rich in old musical authors, and in old compositions, than any one that I have yet seen in Europe. M. de Visme, the day after my arrival, not only sent his secretary with me to the librarian, in the morning, but did me the honour of going to the
library

library with me himſelf after dinner.

The books I wanted were not claſſed under one head, in the general catalogue; but mixt with mathematics and other arts; it was neceſſary, therefore, before I began to ſeek, and examine theſe books, to draw them out of the miſcella-neous catalogue : the reader will form ſome judgment of the number of muſical authors, when he is informed that the liſt of their works only, when extracted from the reſt, filled near twenty large folio ſheets of paper; and theſe are chiefly confined to the ſixteenth century. There were few books of any kind printed in the fifteenth, and ſince the ſixteenth this library has received but a ſmall augmen-tation ; in the chapel, however, there is an immenſe quantity of manuſcript mu-ſic, from the earlieſt time of counter-point to the preſent.

NYMPHENBERG.

During summer the court usually refides here; it is a magnificent *Chateau,* belonging to the Elector, three miles from Munich, where the principal muficians attend, and where his ferene highnefs has a concert every evening.

On my arrival at Munich I had the pleafure of meeting with M. Naumann, the celebrated *maeftro di capella* of the Elector of Saxony, who was brought up in Italy, and who was now on his way thither, to compofe an opera for Venice, and another for Naples. He did me the favour to call on me, and to carry me, on Wednefday morning, to Nymphenberg, where I was engaged to dine with Signor Guadagni. During our ride I obtained from M. Naumann an account of the prefent ftate of mufic in Saxony, from which court he was juft come. At Nymphenberg he attended the rehearfals of the

Electrefs

Electrefs dowager of Saxony's opera of *Taleſtri*, which was on the point of being performed at court, and in which Signor Guadagni was to ſing. Here I found M. Kröner, the Elector's firſt violin, Rauzzini, and Panzachi, who, as well as M. Naumann and myſelf, dined with Guadagni.

The gardens of this *Chateau* are reckoned the fineſt in Germany, and are really as beautiful as they can be made, with innumerable fountains, canals, *jets d'eau,* caſcades, alleys, boſquets, ſtrait rows of trees, and woods, where, " Grove nods at grove," in the true French ſtyle.

There is a beautiful porcelain manufacture at Nymphenberg, which the Bavarians ſay rivals that of Dreſden.

Upon my arrival here, I was informed by Signor Guadagni that he had mentioned me, and the buſineſs I was upon, to the Electrefs dowager of Saxony, and to the Elector, and had arranged every thing for my being preſented to that princeſs before dinner, and to his

Elec-

Electoral highnefs, and the reft of the family, afterwards. Accordingly, about half an hour paft one, a page came to acquaint us that the Electrefs dowager was ready to receive us; and I was conducted through a great number of moft magnificent apartments, by Signor Guadagni, to an anti-chamber, where we waited but a very fhort time, before the Electrefs entered the *Sale d'Audience,* into which we were called, and I was very gracioufly received.

I had enquired into the *Etiquette* of this ceremonial: I was to bend the left knee upon being admitted to the honour of kiffing her hand; after this was over, her highnefs entered into converfation with me in the moft condefcending and eafy manner imaginable; fhe was pleafed to fpeak very favourably of my undertaking, and to add, " that it was not only " doing honour to mufic, but to myfelf, " as fhe believed I was the only modern " hiftorian who thought it neceffary to " travel, in order to gain information at
                                    " the

" the fource, without contenting myfelf
" with fecond-hand, and hear-fay ac-
" counts." This ftrong compliment,
joined to her gracious and pleafing manner, took off all reftraint; fhe was juft
returned from Italy, where, fhe faid, that
" By the great hurry and fatigue of tra-
" velling and talking lord, as is cufto-
" mary at the *Converfazioni* there, fhe
" had almoft totally loft her voice, which
" had been much debilitated before, by
" having had a numerous family, and
" feveral very fevere fits of ficknefs."

Guadagni had told me that her highnefs
fpoke Englifh pretty well, and underftood
it perfectly. I ventured, after fome time,
to entreat her to converfe in the language
of my country, which, I had been informed, fhe had honoured fo far as to
ftudy. She complied with my requeft,
for a fhort time, and fpoke very intelli-
gibly; but faid that fhe had learned it
of an Irifhman, who had given her a vicious pronunciation; which, with the

K 3   few

few opportunities she had for practice,
made it impossible for her to speak well;
but added, that she both read and wrote
English constantly every day, and had great
pleasure in the perusal of our authors.

I then said that I had seen a great
work, both in poetry and music, by her
highness, in England, meaning her opera
of *Talestri*, in which she had united those
arts which had been so long separated.
This produced a musical conversation,
which I wanted, and in the course of
it she said that she could not possibly sit
idle; hers was an active mind, and since
she had ceased to have matters of more
importance upon her hands, she had attached herself seriously to the arts. She
then asked my opinion of the compara-
tive merit of Guadagni, and several great
singers of Italy: he was out of hearing.
She said that Guadagni sung with much
art, as well as feeling; and had the great
secret of hiding defects.

She

She told me that fhe would try to prevail
on her brother, the Elector, to play on
the *viol da gamba* at night; adding, that he
was a good performer, for one who was not
a profeffor; but that we had a very great
player upon that inftrument in England,
M. Abel, with whom I muft not compare him; and added, *nous autres*, " We,
" who are only *Dilettanti*, can never ex-
" pect to equal mafters; for, with the
" fame genius, we want application and
" experience." After this, and fome
farther converfation, I had again the honour, when I retired, of kiffing her hand.

After dining at Guadagni's, I was carried into the *grande fale*, where the Elector, his family, and his court dined, and
were ftill at table. It is one of the fineft
rooms I ever faw. I was glad to find M.
de Vifme of the company; he had been
fo kind as to fpeak of me to the Elector,
and to the Electrefs dowager of Saxony,
which, with what Guadagni had already
done, prepared every thing for my re-

K 4 ception;

ception ; fo that when his highnefs got
up from table, his fifter of Saxony treated
me as one defcended from the *Saxon Race.*
For as foon as fhe had difcovered that I
was in the room, fhe mentioned me to the
Elector, and brought him towards me,
Here I had the honour to kifs his hand,
and had a fhort converfation with him. I
was then prefented to the Electrefs, and
the Margravine of Baden ; after which I
returned to the Elector and his fifter, the
Electrefs dowager, and had a long converfation with them.

The Elector is a very handfome and
gracious prince, has an elegant appearance, and a figure which is neither too
fat, too lean, too tall, nor too fhort,
if I was not too much dazzled by his
condefcenfion, to fee any of his defects. He told his fifter that he fuppofed I could not fpeak German, and
that fhe, therefore, who fpoke Englifh,
muft ferve as my interpreter ; but fhe
faid that as I fpoke French and Italian,
there was no occafion for that flow method

thod of converfation. Upon which his
highnefs began to talk to me in French,
He told me that mine was a very uncommon
journey, and afked, if I was fatisfied with
what materials I had hitherto found.
This afforded me an opportunity of telling him, what was moft true, that in
point of books on my fubject, and ancient
mufic, I had as yet met with nothing
equal to his electoral highnefs's library;
and I had reafon, from the reputation of
the performers, and eminent muficians
in his fervice, to expect great fatisfaction,
as to modern practical mufic. You will
hear fome of them to-night, faid the
Electrefs dowager, and I hope my brother will play, who, for one that is not
a profeffor, fometimes plays very well.
The Elector, in revenge, told me, that his
fifter was both a compofer and a finger.

At this time fome wild beafts were
brought to the palace gates, which all
the company running to fee, put an end,
for the prefent, to our converfation.

This

This was wholly a musical day; for
after dinner, even in seeing the gardens
and buildings, Guadagni and Rauzzini
sung a great part of the time, particularly
in the bath, where there was an excellent
room for music; here they went succes-
fully through all Tartini's experiments,
in order to produce the *third sound*.

At eight o'clock the Elector's band
assembled, for his private concert. The
Electress of Bavaria, and the ladies of
the court were at cards, in the music
room: the concert was begun by two
symphonies of Schwindl; M. Kröner,
who played the first violin, is rather a
bold strong leader of an orchestra than a
solo player. The first song was sung by
Signor Panzachi, who has a good tenor
voice, a pleasing expression, and a facility
of execution: he is likewise said to be
an admirable actor.

After this song, the Electress dowager of Saxony sung a whole scene in
her own opera of *Talestri*; M. Naumann accompanied her on the harpsi-

I   chord,

chord, and the Elector played the violin with Kröner. She fung in a truly fine ftyle; her voice is very weak, but fhe never forces it, or fings out of tune. She fpoke the recitative, which was an accompanied one, very well, in the way of great old fingers of better times. She had been a long while a fcholar of Porpora, who lived many years at Drefden, in the fervice of her father-in-law, Auguftus, king of Poland. This recitative was as well written as it was well expreffed; the air was an *Andante*, rich in harmony, fomewhat in the way of Handel's beft opera fongs in that time. Though there were but few violins, in this concert they were too powerful for the voice, which is a fault that all the fingers of this place complain of.

After this the Elector played one of Schwindl's trios on his *Viol da gamba*, charmingly: except Mr. Abel, I never heard fo fine a player on that inftrument; his hand is firm and brilliant, his tafte and expreffion are admirable, and his fteadi-
nefs

nefs in time, fuch as a *Dilettanti* is feldom poffeffed of.

Rauzzini had, in an obliging manner,
thrown himfelf in the Elector's way, on
purpofe to be afked to fing, that I might
hear him, which I had expreffed a great
defire to do, with a band : for though he
is firft finger, at the ferious opera, in winter, yet he never performs at the fummer
concerts, unlefs particularly defired. He
fung an air of his own compofition admirably well ; then Guadagni fung a pathetic air by Traetta, with his ufual grace
and expreffion, but with more voice than
he had when in England.

The concert concluded with another
piece, performed by the Elector, with ftill
more tafte and expreffion than the firft, efpecially the *Adagio*. I could not praife it fufficiently ; it would really have been thought
excellently well performed, if, inftead of
a great prince, he had been a mufician by
profeffion. I could only tell his highnefs, that I was aftonifhed as much as
if I had never before heard how great a
performer he was.

After

After this, his highnefs and the court fupped in the fame great hall and public manner, in which they had dined. I went with Guadagni, and the reft of the principal performers, to make my court during the fupper. The Elector was pleafed to fpeak a confiderable time to Guadagni, concerning my future Hiftory of Mufic; which encouraged me to defire him to entreat his highnefs, to honour me with a piece of his compofition, as I had been informed by all the muficians of this place, that he had compofed feveral excellent things for the church, particularly, a *Stabat Mater:* he agreed to give me a *Litany*, provided I would not print it; but Guadagni quite teazed him to let me have the *Stabat Mater*, as he faid, it was the beft of all his mufical productions; and even a promife of this was granted before my departure *.

* Both thefe compofitions were tranfcribed for me, after I left Munich, and delivered to M. de Vifme, by whofe care and kindnefs they have been fince tranfmitted to me in London.

2   The

The lords in waiting offered us re-
freshments; and the Elector condefcended to afk Guadagni, if he gave a fupper
to the Englifhman, and his other company? meaning Panzachi, Rauzzini, and
Naumann; he anfwered, that he fhould
give us bread and cheefe, and a glafs of
wine. "Here," cried the Elector, emptying
two difhes of game on a plate, " fend that
" to your apartments." His highnefs
was implicitly obeyed. We fupped together, after which I returned to Munich, abundantly flattered and fatisfied
with the events of the day.

MUNICH.

The next morning was fpent in the library. I had afterwards the pleafure of
dining with Signora Mingotti, who invited to meet me, father Kenedy, a worthy Scotfman, of real parts and learning.
After dinner, a long and fpirited converfation took place; for the lady is animated, eloquent, and well informed:

she

ſhe related her adventures in Spain, and other parts of the world, and interſperſed them with reflections concerning muſic, upon which it is impoſſible to hear her ſpeak unimproved, as ſhe treats the ſubject with uncommon depth, preciſion, and perſpicuity.

From hence I went to ſee the Elector's theatre, where his ſerious operas are performed in winter. It is not large, having but four rows of boxes, fifteen in each ; but it is more richly fitted up, than any that I had ever ſeen.

On Thurſday, father Kenedy was ſo obliging, as to carry me to the academy, where he ſhewed me all that was worthy of notice, in machines, mathematical inſtruments, models, minerals, foſſils, and other curioſities ; but what moſt attracted my attention, as coming neareſt to my *buſineſs*, if not my *boſom*, was a collection of thirty-ſix thouſand tracts and diſſertations on different ſubjects, bound up in near nine hundred volumes ;

they

they were bought for the prefent Elector, at Leipfic. There is an index of authors, but as yet, none completed of things; there is one begun, but it goes no farther than the letter M, and this father Kenedy, who is at the head of the academy, was fo obliging as to lend me. This inftitution has not been founded above eleven years; however, several volumes of its Tranfactions are already printed, and it feems, at prefent, to be carried on with fpirit.

To-day I had the honour of dining with M. de Vifme, who after dinner, was fo kind as to go with me to the Jefuit's college, where I had a very particular enquiry to make, which not only concerned the Hiftory of Mufic, but its prefent ftate. In my progrefs through Germany, I had frequently heard mufic performed in the churches, and ftreets by *poor fcholars,* as they were always called, but never could make out how, or by whom they were taught, till on

my

my arrival here. M. de Vifme, who neglected to inform me of nothing, which in the leaft related to my defign, told me, that there was a *mufic fchool* at the Jefuits college. This awakened my curiofity, and made me fufpect, that it was a kind of *Confervatorio*; and, upon a more minute enquiry, I found, that the *poor fcholars* whom I had heard fing, in fo many different parts of Germany, had been taught, in each place, where the Roman catholic religion prevailed, at the Jefuits college; and, further, I was informed, that in all the towns throughout the empire, where the Jefuits have a church or college, young perfons are taught to play upon mufical inftruments, and to fing. Many muficians have been brought up here, who afterwards have rendered themfelves eminent. This will, in fome meafure account for the great number of mufi-cians, with which Germany abounds, as

L   well

well as for the national taſte and paſſion
for muſic.

The muſic ſchool in Munich takes in
eighty children, at about eleven or twelve
years old; they are taught muſic, read-
ing, and writing, and are boarded, but
not cloathed. A Jeſuit, to whom we
applied for information, promiſed to write
down, in Latin, an account of this foundation, as far as it might be neceſſary to
the Hiſtory of Muſic in Germany, and
ſend it to M. de Viſme next day; and he
kept his word. The boys that are admitted here, in order to be taught muſic,
muſt play upon ſome inſtrument, or know
ſomething of the art, to qualify them for
admittance. They are kept in the college till twenty years of age; and, during
the time of their reſidence there, they are
taught by maſters of the town, not by the
Jeſuits themſelves.

There are others, under the denomination of *poor ſcholars,* who are intended

for

for the church, and who are taught the learned languages, mathematics, and theology.

From hence I went to the burletta of *Le Finte Gemelli, Farza per mufica, à quat-tro voci,* fet by Matteo Raúzzini, bro-ther to the finger of that name, a young man of only eighteen years of age. The mufic was moft of it common, but pretty, and in good tafte. The Lodi fung charm-ingly; her voice and figure would make her a capital finger in a ferious opera, if fhe were well taught. Her voice wants only a little more room in its paffage through the throat; in every thing elfe, fhe is admirable; having a pretty figure, a good expreffion, and an exquifite man-ner of taking *appogiature.*

The fecond finger of this company, Signora Manfervifi, deferves to be men-tioned; her figure is agreeable, her voice, though not ftrong, is well-toned, fhe has nothing vulgar in her manner, fings in tune, and never gives offence.

L 2   There

There was a tenor, Signor Fiorini, who fung to-night, whom I had not heard before; he has perhaps been a better finger than he is at prefent; but now, neither his voice, nor manner, had any thing interefting in it, though both were free from any common defects; for he fung in tune, had a fhake, and was far from vulgar.

In going home from the opera, I heard a very good concert in the ftreet; it was performed at the door of M. de Vifme, by torch-light, and attended by a great crowd: after I returned to my lodgings, I heard the fame performers at the inn door; upon enquiring who they were, I was told, that they were *poor fcholars*; but I did not difcover till the next day, that this concert was intended, as a regale, for M. de Vifme and me, on account of our having been at their college to inform ourfelves concerning their inftitution.

Friday. I fpent the greateft part of this morning with Signor Rauzzini; he

was

was fo obliging as to fing to me a great number of excellent fongs, in different ftyles, among which there were many of his own compofition. As to his abilities in finging, I think his fhake is not quite open enough, nor did I then think his voice fufficiently powerful for a great theatre; but in all other refpects he is a charming performer; his tafte is quite modern and delicate; the tone of his voice fweet and clear; his execution of paffages of the moft difficult intonation amazingly neat, rapid, and free: and his knowledge of harmony is far beyond that of any great ftage-finger I ever knew: he has likewife a very good perfon, and, I am told, is an excellent actor.

The reft of this day was employed in the Elector's, and in other libraries. At night I heard the *poor fcholars* again in the ftreets, where they performed fome full pieces very well: there were violins, hautboys, French horns, a violoncello, and baffoon. I was informed, that they

L 3   were

were obliged frequently to perform thus in the ftreets, to convince the public, at whofe expence they are maintained, of the proficiency they make.

Saturday 22d. I was this whole morning at Signora Mingotti's, from whom I obtained, in converfation, a fketch of her mufical life. I am doubtful as to the propriety of publifhing thefe anecdotes; however, as no fecrecy was enjoined, and as they contain nothing difgraceful to the perfon who furnifhed them, I fhall venture to do it, fuppofing a curiofity concerning the moft trivial circumftances, relative to eminent perfons, to be as ftrong in others as in myfelf,

Her parents were Germans; her father was an officer in the Auftrian fervice, who being called to Naples, upon duty, his wife travelled with him thither during her pregnancy, and was there brought to bed of this daughter; who, however, was carried to Gratz, in Silefia, before

fhe

ſhe was a year old; and her father dying
while ſhe was young, her uncle placed
her in a convent of Urſulines, where ſhe
was educated, and where ſhe received
her firſt leſſons of muſic.

She told me, that during her child-
hood, ſhe remembers being ſo pleaſed
with the muſic performed in the chapel
of her convent, particularly with a Litany ſung there one feſtival, that ſhe
went to the abbeſs, with tears in her eyes,
and trembling, both with fear of anger, and
of a refuſal, to intreat her to teach her
to ſing, as *ſhe* did in the chapel. The
abbeſs put her off, with ſaying, that ſhe
was very buſy that day, but would think
of it. The next day ſhe ſent one of
the elder nuns to aſk her who bid her
make that requeſt, when the little Regina (as ſhe was then called) replied,
that nobody had bid her, but that it was
merely her own love for muſic, which
inſpired the thought. After this the
abbeſs ſent for her, and told her, that

ſhe

she had very little time to spare; but, if she would promise to be diligent, she would teach her herself; adding, that she could only afford her half an hour à day; but with that, she would soon find what her genius and induſtry were likely to produce, and she should go on with, or diſcontinue, her inſtructions, accordingly.

Regina was in rapture with this compliance of the abbeſs, who began to inſtruct her the next day, *à table ſec*, as she expreſſed it, without a harpſichord, or any other inſtrument *.

In this manner she was taught the elements of muſic, and *ſolfeggi*, with the principles of harmony, and was obliged to ſing the treble, while the abbeſs ſung the baſe. She shewed me a very ſmall

---

* She applied herſelf to the harpſichord ſeveral years after, and ſtill accompanies upon it very well. But it was perhaps owing to her manner of learning to ſing *without* an inſtrument, that she acquired the firmneſs in her performance, for which she has always been remarkable.

book,

book, in which all her firſt leſſons were written; the explanations were in the German language.

She remained in this convent till ſhe had attained her fourteenth year, at which time, upon the death of her uncle, ſhe went home to her mother. During the life of her uncle, ſhe had been intended for the veil. When ſhe quitted the convent, ſhe appeared, in the eyes of her mother and ſiſters, to be one of the moſt uſeleſs and helpleſs of beings; they looked upon her as a fine lady, brought up in a boarding ſchool, without knowing any thing of houſhold concerns; and her mother neither knew what to do with her, or her fine voice, which both ſhe and her ſiſters deſpiſed, not foreſeeing that it would one day be productive of ſo much honour and profit to the poſſeſſor.

Not many years after ſhe quitted the convent, Signor Mingotti, an old Venetian, and manager of the opera at Dreſden, was propoſed as a huſband for her.
She

She detested him, but was at length worried into a compliance, which was the sooner extorted from her, perhaps, as she, like other young women, imagined that by losing, she should gain her liberty.

People talked very much of her fine voice, and manner of singing. Porpora was at this time in the late king of Poland's service, at Dresden : he had heard her sing, and spoke of her at court as a young person of great expectations; which occasioned a proposal to her husband for her entering into the service of the Elector : he had before marriage promised never to suffer her to sing on the stage ; however, he came home one day, and asked her, if she should like to engage in the service of the court. She thought this was done in derision, and gave him a short and peevish answer ; but he continuing to teize her on the subject, at length convinced her that he was in earnest, and had a commission to treat with her. She liked the thoughts of sing-finging, and turning her voice to fome account, and therefore gladly entered into articles for a fmall ftipend, not above three or four hundred crowns a year.

When her voice had been heard at court, it was fuppofed to raife a jealoufy in Fauftina, who was then in that fervice, but upon the point of retiring; and confequently in Haffe, her hufband, particularly when he heard that Porpora, his old and conftant rival, was to have a hundred crowns a month for teaching her. He faid it was Porpora's laft ftake; the only twig he had to catch at; *un clou pour s'accrocher*. However, her talents made fuch a noife at Drefden, that the fame of them reached Naples, to which place fhe was invited, to fing at the great theatre. At this time fhe knew but little Italian; however, fhe now went ferioufly to work in ftudying it.

The firft character fhe appeared in was *Ariftæa*, in the opera of the *Olimpiade*, fet by Galuppi. Montecelli performed

the part of *Megacles*. On this occasion
her talents, as an actress, gained her as
much applause as her singing : she was
bold and enterprising ; and, seeing the
character in a different light from what
others had done before her, would, in
spite of the advice of old actors, who
durst not deviate from custom, play it in
a way quite different from any one of
her predecessors. It was in this original
and courageous manner that Mr. Garrick
first surprised and charmed an English
audience ; and, in defiance of contracted
rules, which had been established by ignorance, prejudice, and want of genius,
struck out a style of speaking and acting,
which the whole nation has ever since
continued to approve with acclamation,
rather than applause.

After this success at Naples, Signora
Mingotti received letters from all parts
of Europe, to offer her terms for engaging at different operas ; but she was not
then at liberty to accept of any of them,
being

being obliged to return to the court of
Drefden, in which fervice fhe was ftill a
penfioner; however, her falary was con-
fiderably augmented, and fhe frequently
expreffes her gratitude to that court, and
fays fhe owes to it all her fame and fortune. Here fhe repeated, with great applaufe, her part in the *Olimpiade*; every
one agreed, that in point of voice, execution, and acting, her powers were very
great; but many thought that fhe was
wholly unfit for any thing pathetic or
tender.

Haffe was now employed to fet *Demo-
foonte* *; and fhe imagined that he kindly
gave her an *Adagio*, accompanied by the
violins, *Pizzicati*, merely to expofe and
fhew her defects. But fufpecting the
fnare, fhe ftudied hard to efcape it;
and in the fong, *Se tutti i Mali Miei*,
which fhe afterwards fung in England,
with great applaufe, fhe fucceeded fo

* This happened in 1748.

well,

well, as to filence even Fauftina herfelf. Sir Ch. H. Williams was Englifh
minifter here at this time, and being in-
timate with Haffe and his wife, had
joined their party, publicly declaring
that Mingotti was utterly unable to fing
a flow and pathetic fong; but when he
had heard her, he made a public recan-
tation, afked her pardon for doubting of
her abilities, and ever after remained her
firm friend and adherent.

From hence fhe went into Spain, where
fhe fung with Gizziello, in the operas
under the direction of Signor Farinelli;
who, fhe told me, was, fo fevere a difci-
plinarian, that he would not allow her
to fing any where but in the opera at
court, or even to practife, in a room
next the ftreet. She was requefted to
fing at private concerts, by many of the
firft nobility and grandees of Spain, but
could not obtain permiffion from the director; who carried his prohibition fo
far, as to deny a pregnant lady, of great
rank,

rank, the fatisfaction of hearing her, though fhe was unable to go to the theatre, and declared that fhe *longed* for a fong from Mingotti. The Spaniards have a religious refpect for thefe involuntary and unruly affections in females thus circumftanced, however they may be treated as problematical in other countries *. The hufband, therefore, of the lady, complained to the king of the cruelty of the opera director, who, he faid, would kill both his wife and child, if his majefty did not interfere. The king lent a favourable ear to the complaint, and ordered Mingotti to receive the lady at her houfe, in which his majefty was implicitly obeyed, the lady's defire was fatisfied, and the child prevented, perhaps, from being marked, in fome part of its body, with a mufic paper, or from having an Italian fong written with indelible characters on its face.

* See *l'Hiftoire Naturelle*, *de* M. de Buffon, tom. ii.

Sig-

Signora Mingotti remained two years
in Spain, from whence she came to England, for the first time. How much she
was then admired, at our opera, is too
recent to need being mentioned here.
She afterwards sung in every great city
of Italy; but she always regarded Dresden as her home, during the life-time of
the Elector Augustus, late king of Poland. She is now settled at Munich,
more, it is thought, from cheapness than
attachment. She has no pension from
this court, as was reported, but, with
œconomy, she has just sufficient, from
her savings, to bring her through the
year. She seems to live very comfortably, to be well received at court, and to
be esteemed by all such as are able to
judge of her understanding, and to enjoy
her conversation.

It gave me great pleasure to hear her
speak concerning practical music, which she
does with as much intelligence as any *maes-
tro di capella* with whom I ever conversed.

2   Her

Her knowledge in finging, and powers of expreffion, in different ftyles, are ftill amazing, and muft delight all fuch as can receive pleafure from fong, unconnected with the blandifhments of youth and beauty. She fpeaks three languages, German, French and Italian, fo well, that it is difficult to fay which of them is her own. Englifh fhe likewife fpeaks, and Spanifh, well enough to converfe in them, and underftands Latin ; but, in the three languages firft mentioned, fhe is truly eloquent.

In the afternoon father Kenedy was fo obliging as to attend me again at the academy; in order to affift in finding fuch tracts, among the great number which are bound up together, as I had marked in the catalogue.

From hence I returned, by appointment, to Signora Mingotti. She had got her harpfichord tuned, and I prevailed on her to fing, to no other accompaniment, for near four hours. It was now

M   that

that I difcovered her fuperior knowledge in finging. She is wholly out of practice, and hates mufic here, fhe fays, as fhe can feldom be well accompanied, or well heard; her voice is, however, much better than when fhe was laft in England.

Prince Sapieha, a Polifh nobleman, and his princefs, lodged at the fame inn as myfelf, the Golden Hart. The prince is very mufical, and plays well on the violin. I had the honour of being known to him a little by living in the fame houfe; but M. de Vifme was fo kind as to explain to him the nature of my mufical enquiries, and to tell him how curious I was after national mufic of all kinds: upon which his highnefs was pleafed to fend me word, that if I would call upon him about nine o'clock, any morning, he would gladly give me a fpecimen of the mufic of his country, as it depended fo much on the *coup d'archet*, that feeing it on paper, without hearing it performed, would afford but a very imperfect idea of it.

The

The day before my departure from Munich, when I had the honour of paying my respects to this prince, he condescended to receive me in a most obliging manner, and to play to me a great number of very pretty Polish pieces, which he executed very well, and to which he gave an expression that was at the same time delicate and singular. He had two German musicians to accompany him in these pieces; the one on the violin, and the other on the violoncello; every movement was in triple time, or $\frac{3}{4}$, with the close constantly on the second note in the bar, instead of the first; but upon my asking if there was no such thing as Polish music, in common time, the prince told me that there were some Cossack tunes in $\frac{4}{2}$, used chiefly in dancing, and he played me some of them. The accompaniment was constantly the $\frac{3}{8}$ and $\frac{4}{8}$, of the key, played a bar full, or four quavers of each, alternately.

M 2

His

His highnefs told me that they have no church mufic in Poland, which is not Italian; and the kind of mufic which we call Polonoife, is played quicker for dancing than at other times. The military mufic of Poland is like that of other countries, confifting only of marches in the ufual time. I enquired after the Polifh inftruments, in order to know if there were any of a different conftruction from ours, but found that they had only guittars and lutes, fomewhat differing in form, and in tuning, from thofe in other parts of Europe. The Poles have no plays, with fongs intermixt, or operas, but fuch as are either French or Italian.

After anfwering thefe queftions, the prince played a very pretty minuet, and two or three Polonoifes of his own compofition; and, upon my expreffing approbation, he was pleafed to make me a prefent of them: he likewife ordered fome of the beft pieces which he had

played

played before, to be tranfcribed for me, which he fent to me at night, together with a fpecimen of Coffack melody; and, when I retired, he condefcended to fay that he fhould be very glad to meet me again, in the courfe of my journey, and to render me every fervice in his power.

Prince Sapieha told me, that he had long had in his fervice an Englifhman, who was an excellent mufician, and of fo good a character, that he had not only made him his *maeftro di capella*, but alfo his *homme de confiance*. He had been brought into Poland very young.

This prince is young and handfome in perfon. He is a diffident, and retired hither, from the troubles and defolation of his country, with his princefs, a fenfible and accomplifhed lady, as I was informed by a perfon who had feveral times converfed with her *.

---

* Since my departure from Munich, his eftates in Poland have been confifcated, by order of the Emprefs of Ruffia, on account of his having refufed to do homage for them to that princefs, and

confefs

I went again to court at Nymphenberg, before my departure, and was again
honoured by the notice of the Elector and
his fifter, and obtained a reiterated promife from both of a piece of mufic of
their compofition. The Elector at firſt
made fome difficulty, left I fhould publifh it; as his *Stabat Mater* had been
ftolen, and printed at Verona, without his
permiſſion, and would have been publifhed, had not his highnefs purchafed the
plates, and the whole impreſſion; but
upon my affuring him that without licence I fhould never make any other ufe
of the piece, with which he fhould honour me, than to enrich my collection of
fcarce and curious compofitions, he was
pleafed to give orders for its being tranfcribed.

The Electrefs dowager told me that
her difpofition, in this particular, was
different from her brother's; for, inſtead

confefs her legal fovereignty to the Polifh territories,
of which, by force of arms, fhe has poffeffed herfelf,

of

of concealing what she was able to produce, she took as much care to have it known, as the birth of a legitimate child; and had, accordingly, printed and published her two operas in score: so that she feared she had nothing left among her papers, worth bestowing; however, she gave Guadagni permission to look them over, and to let me have whatever he thought best worth my acceptance.

After this I had the honour of being presented, by M. de Vismе, to the Dutchess of Bavaria, the widow of the Elector's brother, and sister to the Electress Palatine of the Rhine; she is of a very pleasing figure and character. It was at the desire of this princess that M. de Vismе called me to her: they had previously been talking of my having been at Manheim and Schwetzingen; and, upon her being told that I had not been presented to her brother, the Elector Palatine, for want of a minister, or proper person at that court, to do me that ho-

M 4　　　　nour,

nour, she expressed great surprize, and indeed concern. She was pleased to say that it would have given her brother great pleasure to have conversed with a person whose pursuits were such as mine, as he was particularly fond of music; and added, that he not only read and spoke English, but had a natural partiality to all who were of my country. I told her highness how I was circumstanced; that I had been favoured with a letter from Mr. Cressener, our minister at Bonn, which had not operated so soon as I could have wished; and that I was too much pressed in time to be able to wait long enough for it to take effect; and added, that all I aspired at in this journey, was to obtain an opportunity of hearing the best performers, and seeing the works of the best composers of Germany, in order to be enabled, in the course of my History of Music, to do justice to their talents and genius. The Dutchess was pleased to say, that she was certain her bro-

brother, the Elector Palatine, would be sorry to find, that I had been at his capital, and at Schwetzingen, without his having been apprized of it.

After this M. de Vifme was fo kind, as to carry me back to Munich as faft as poffible, in order to attend at a concert, which Signora Mingotti obligingly made for me, of the beft muficians which fhe could get together upon fhort notice, whom I had not heard before. M. Kröner, whofe performance I had only heard at Nymphenburg in full pieces, was firft violin. There was M. Sechi, a very good hautboy, who, if I had not lately heard Fifcher, would have charmed me; M. Rheiner, the baffoon, who, when in England, was fo ill, that he was unable to play more than once in public, and whom I had not yet heard, was here tonight, and had quite recovered his health. His tone is fweet, and execution neat, and he muft be allowed by every compe-

tent

tent and impartial judge, to be a very able and pleasing performer.

Madame la Presidente, a lady of fashion, a friend and neighbour of Signora Mingotti, opened the concert, by a lesson on the harpsichord, which she executed with uncommon rapidity and precision. A *quintetto* was played next, that was composed by M. Michel, a young man that had been brought up at the Jesuit's music school.   He has a genius, that wants only the pruning knife of time and experience to lop off luxuriance; every performer in this piece had an opportunity of shewing the genius of his instrument, and his own powers of execution. There was, in the solo parts, the brilliant, pathetic, and graceful, by turns; and the *tutti* parts had no other imperfection, than being too learned, and *recherchées* in modulation.   I hardly ever heard a composition, that discovered more genius and invention, one that required

quired more abilities in the execution, or that was better performed; it was made for a violin, a hautboy, tenor, baffoon, and violoncello.

Signor Guadagni and Signor Rauzzini were both at this concert, and the latter, whom I had only heard before, in one fong, with full accompaniments, was fo obliging, as to fing a very pretty air of his own compofition, and another admirable one, by Signor Sacchini, in the *Eroc Cinefe*. In the execution of thefe airs, he manifefted great and captivating powers: a fweet and extenfive voice, a rapid brilliancy of execution, great expreffion, and an exquifite and judicious tafte. I was to-day even furprifed by the ftrength of his voice, which had before appeared rather too feeble for a great theatre; but it was want of exertion, for now it made its way through all the inftruments, when playing *fortiffimo*.

A duet by Sechi and Rheiner, which finifhed the concert, put me in mind of
the

the two Bezozzis, at Turin; as their inftruments, fo their genius and abilities
feem made for each other, there being
a like correfpondence in both.

After thefe charming performances were
over, I haftened to the comic opera, at
which were the Elector, and all the electoral family. Count Seeau, intendant of
the Elector's mufic, had moft obligingly
changed the opera, in order to afford me
an opportunity of hearing Signora Lodi
in her beft character. The burletta of
to-night was the *Moglie Fedele*, compofed
by Signor Guglielmi; her voice is brilliant, and ftyle of finging charming;
but as I had, in London, feen Signora
Guadagni in the fame character, her
acting did not ftrike me fo much as
it would otherwife have done. After the
opera, there was a long dance, which
was an ingenious and entertaining pantomime, and of which, the fcenes and
decorations were well contrived, and
fplendid.

The

The next day, which was that of my departure from Munich, at nine o'clock in the morning, Signora Mingotti, who was indefatigable in rendering me every service in her power, had prepared another small, but select band, for me at her house, in order to afford me an opportunity of hearing two scholars of Tartini on the violin; M. Holtzbogn, and Lobst, which political reasons had prevented her from inviting the day before. They are both good performers; had been in the service of the late duke of Bavaria, and have still a pension, though but few opportunities of being heard.

Holtzbogn has a great hand, a clear tone, and more fire than is usual, in one of the Tartini school, which is rather remarkable for delicacy, expression, and high finishing, than for spirit and variety. This performer writes well for his instrument, and played a very masterly concerto of his own composition. Lobst played a concerto of Tartini with great delicacy;

delicacy; he is naturally timid, and want
of practice added nothing to his courage;
however, through these difadvantages,
he difcovered himfelf to be a worthy
difciple of the great Tartini.

After thefe pieces Signora Rofa Capra-
nica, in the fervice of this court, and fcholar of Signora Mingotti, brought hither
from Rome by the Electrefs dowager of
Saxony, fung a very difficult fong by
Traetta, with great neatnefs, and in a pleafing and agreeable manner. This performer is young, and has natural powers
capable of great things, at which if fhe
does not arrive, under fuch a miftrefs as
Signora Mingotti, it muft be totally attributed to want of diligence.

The city of Munich is one of the beft
built, and moft beautiful in Germany;
I am afhamed to mention all the honours
and favours, which were undefervedly
conferred upon me, during my fhort refidence there. All that I can add to this
article is, that I quitted it with great re-
gret;

gret; as I had fo numerous an acquaintance, and fo many proteƈtors, that I
lamented the not being able to fpare
more time, to avail myfelf of their kindnefs and good offices.

*　　*　　*　　*

I went from Munich to Vienna, down
the two rivers Ifer and Danube; and
as the mufical incidents during this voyage are but few, and no itinerary or book
of travels, that I remember to have feen,
has defcribed the courfe of thefe rivers,
or the method by which perfons are conveyed upon them, from one place to
another, I fhall not fcruple to add to my
few mufical memorandums, fuch other
remarks and obfervations as I find fet
down in my mifcellaneous journal.

The Ifer, upon which the city of Munich is fituated, and which empties itfelf
into the Danube, about a hundred miles
below, though very rapid, is too much
fpread and fcattered into different chan-
nels, to be fufficiently deep for a bark,

I

or any kind of paſſage-boat, that has a
bottom to float upon it. The current of
this river is even too rapid for any thing to
be brought back againſt it; but Bavaria being a country abounding with wood, particularly fir, rafts, or floats made of thoſe
trees, laſhed together, are carried down
the ſtream, at the rate of ſeventy or
eighty miles a day. Upon theſe rafts, a
booth is built for paſſengers in common;
but if any one chuſes to have a cabin to
himſelf, he may have it built for about
four florins. I preferred this, not only
to avoid bad company and heat, but to
get an opportunity of writing and di-
geſting my thoughts and memorandums,
being at this time very much in arrears
with my muſical journal.

I quitted Munich at two o'clock in
the afternoon. The weather was in-
tenſely hot, and I was furniſhed with
no means of tempering it; a clear ſky
and burning ſun, reflected from the water, having rendered my fir cabin as in-
ſupportable as the open air. It was conſtructed

conſtructed of green boards, which ex-
uded as much turpentine as would have
vanquiſhed all the aromatics of Arabia.

As I was utterly ignorant of the country, through which I was to paſs, and
the accommodations it would afford, all
that my foreſight had ſuggeſted to me,
in the way of furniture and proviſions,
were a mattreſs, blanket, and ſheets;
ſome cold meat, with bread, and a bottle
of wine; there was water in plenty
always at hand. But I ſoon found myſelf in want of many other things; and,
if I were ever to perform this voyage
again, which I hope will never happen,
experience would enable me to render
the cabin a tolerable reſidence, for a
week or ten days.

In quitting Munich by water, the city
is a beautiful object; but the country
we paſſed through is a wretched one, to
all appearance; there being nothing but
willows, ſedge, ſand, and gravel in
ſight. The water was ſo ſhallow in ſe-
N   veral

veral places, that I thought our float
would have ſtuck faſt. At ſix o'clock
we arrived at Freiſing, the ſee and ſove-
reignty of a prince biſhop; his palace is
placed on a high hill at a little diſtance
from the town, which is on another hill,
and looks very pretty from the water-
ſide. I would not go on ſhore to pay for a
bad bed and ſupper, with which I was
already furniſhed in my cabin; my ſervant
however went with the common company, which amounted to upwards of fifty
perſons, in order to get ſome freſh bread,
but which the place did not afford.

There had been no rain in theſe parts
of Germany for ſix weeks; but, when we
arrived at Freiſing, I ſaw a little black cloud
to the weſtward, which, in leſs than half
an hour, produced the moſt violent ſtorm
of thunder, lightning, rain, and wind,
that I ever remember to have ſeen. I
really expected every moment, that the
lightning would have ſet fire to my cabin; it continued all night with prodigious

gious fury, fo that my man could not get back, and I was left on the water, fole inhabitant of the float, which was fecured by a hawfer to a wooden-bridge.

Two fquare holes were cut in the boards of my cabin, one on each fide, by way of window; the pieces were to ferve as cafements, one of thefe was loft, fo that I was forced to faften with pins, a handkerchief againft the hole, to keep out wind and rain; but it anfwered the purpofe very ill, and moreover, it rained in, at a hundred different places; drop, drip, drop, throughout my little habitation, fometimes on my face, fometimes on my legs, and always fomewhere or other. This, with the violent flafhes of lightning and burfts of thunder, kept off drowfinefs; luckily, perhaps, for I might have caught cold, fleeping in the wet. I had been told, that the people of Bavaria were, at leaft, three hundred years behind the reft of Europe in philofophy, and ufeful knowledge. No-

N 2   thing

thing can cure them of the folly of ring-
ing the bells whenever it thunders, or
perfuade them to put up conductors to
their public buildings; though the lightning here is fo mifchievous, that laft
year, no lefs than thirteen churches were
deftroyed by it, in the electorate of Bavaria. The recollection of this, had not
the effect of an opiate upon me; the bells
in the town of Freifing were jingling
the whole night, to remind me of their
fears, and the real danger I was in. I
lay on the mattrefs, as far as I could from
my fword, piftols, watch-chain, and
every thing that might ferve as a conductor. I never was much frightened
by lightning before, but now I wifhed
for one of Dr. Franklin's beds, fufpend-
ed by filk cords in the middle of a large
room. I weathered it out till morning,
without a wink of fleep; my fervant
told me, that the inn on fhore was mi-
ferable; it rained into every room of the
houfe, and no provifions could be found

2   for

for thefe fifty people, but black bread and beer, boiled up with two or three eggs.

At fix, we got into motion, the rain and wind continuing with great fury, and from violent heat, the air grew fo chill and cold, that I found it impoffible to keep myfelf warm with all the things I could put on. For though I added to my drefs a pair of thick fhoes, woollen ftockings, a flannel waiftcoat, great-coat and night-cap, with all the warm garments in my poffeffion, yet I was benumbed with cold.

We advanced for four hours through a dreary country, as far as I was able to defcry, but the weather was fo bad, that I could not often examine it. At ten o'clock fome fir trees appeared, which enlivened the view, and at eleven, nothing elfe could be feen on either fide. There was a very high and fteep fhore on the right, covered with firs, and on the left, trees fcattered near the water, and groves at a diftance. At eleven, the float ftopped

N 3

at

at Landſhut, where the paſſengers dined.
I ſtuck to my cabin and cold meat: if it
had not rained in, I ſhould have thought
myſelf very well off; but, in my preſent
circumſtances I was ſo uncomfortable,
that I could not, for a long time, write a
word in my journal books; the weather
had ſo lowered my ſpirits, and ſtiffened
my fingers; however, towards the afternoon, I made an effort, and tranſcribed
many things from my tablets, which
were full. At ſix o'clock, the float ſtopt
at Dingelſing; in the evening I got a
candle, which was a luxury denied to
me the night before in the thunder-ſtorm.
Rain, rain, eternal rain, and wind made
the water nothing leſs than pleaſant.

The next morning was clear, but cold.
The paſſengers landed at Landau about
ten; at one we entered the Danube,
which did not appear ſo vaſt a river here
as I expected. However, it grew larger
as we deſcended; we ſtopt at two o'clock
at a miſerable village, with a fine convent in it, however. Here the wind became

came fo violent, that I thought every
minute it would have carried away both
my cabin and myfelf; at three, it was
determined to ftay here all night, as it
was not fafe to ftir during this wind;
but as this feems, and is called, *Le
Païs des vents*, it was an excercife for
patience to be ftopt at a place, where
I had nothing to do. My provifions
grew fhort and ftale, and there were
none of any kind to be had here!

I had fuffered fo much the night before,
that I now ferioufly fet about contriving
how to keep myfelf warm. The blanket
bought at Munich for me, by my knave,
or fool of a fervant, and which I had
not feen foon enough to change, was a
fecond-hand one, and fo filthy, ragged,
and likely to contain all kinds of vermin,
and perhaps difeafes, that hitherto I
could not find in my heart to touch it;
however, cold and hunger will tame
the proudeft ftomachs. I put the blan-

ket

ket over the sheet, and was gladdened
by its warmth.

At three in the morning, the paf-
fengers were called, and soon after the
float was in motion; it was now a huge
and unwieldy machine, a quarter of a
mile long, and loaded with deals, hogf-
heads, and lumber of all kinds. The
sun rose very bright; but at six there
was a strong easterly wind, full in our
teeth, and so great a fog, that not a
single object could be seen on either side
the river.

When I agreed to live night and day,
for a week, upon the water, I forgot to
bargain for warm weather; and now it
was so cold, that I could scarcely hold
the pen, though but the 27th of August!
I have often observed, that when the
body is cold, the mind is chilled likewife; and this was now so much the cafe
with myself, that I had neither spirits
nor ideas for working at my musical
journal.

At

At eight o'clock we ſtopt at Vilſcho-
fen, a ſweet ſituation. Here is a wooden
bridge, of ſixteen arches, over the Danube. The hills on the oppoſite ſide of
the town are covered with wood, and
exceedingly beautiful. The fog was diſ-
ſipated, and the ſun now ſhone on them
in great glory. There is a gentle viſit here
from the cuſtom-houſe officers; the ſeals
were cut off my trunk, being the laſt
town in Bavaria. They threatened hard
as to the ſevere examination I was to
undergo upon entering Auſtria; however,
I had little to loſe, except time; and that
was now too precious to be patiently
parted with to theſe inquiſitorial robbers.

At half an hour paſt nine we ſet off
for Paſſau, in very fine weather, which
revived my ſpirits, and enabled me to
hold my pen. The Danube abounds in
rocks, ſome above water, and ſome below, which occaſion a great noiſe by the
rapidity of the current, running over, or
againſt them.

We

We met this morning a gang of boats, laden with falt, from Saltzburg and Paffau, dragged up the river by more than forty horfes, a man on each, which expence is fo great, as to enhance the price of that commodity above four hundred per cent. We did not feem to move fo faft now as upon the Ifer, which had frequent cafcades; and fometimes the float dipped fo deep, as to have three or four feet of water rufh fuddenly into my cabin.

P A S S A U.

This is the boldeft, and at the fame time the pleafanteft fituation, that I ever faw. The town is built on the fide and fummit of a fteep hill, on the right of the Danube. There is a hill on the other fide, anfwering to that on which the town is built; however, there are but few houfes upon it.

Paffau is a large imperial city. In the cathedral, which is a very beautiful modern

dern building, of the Corinthian order, there is a very magnificent organ, to look at. The case is finely carved and gilt, and the pipes are highly polished: it is divided into two columns of large pipes, one on each side, and has a complete little organ in the middle, which joins them together, and saves the west window: it is what builders call a thirty-two foot organ. M. Snetzler, when it was last repaired, made some of the front pipes, but there is little variety in the inside: he likewise made the *vox humana*, and octave *dulciana*, in the little organ, which are the two best solo stops that the instrument contains.

On each side of the choir, in this church, there is likewise a small organ, with the pipes so highly burnished, that I cannot help supposing them to be of silver: indeed the person who shewed me the great one, assured me that they were silver pipes; but as he likewise would have persuaded me that the front of the great organ was of that metal, in which

I was certain he was miftaken, I cannot
depend on his word.

At the end of this town is the con-
fluence of three rivers; the *Inn*, on the
right hand; the *Iltz*, on the left; and
the *Danube* in the middle. After this
junction, the Danube becomes more and
more rapid: the fhore on each fide, for
a confiderable way below Paffau, has hills
and rocks as high as thofe at Briftol;
but thefe are covered with fpruce fir
trees and box, and look much lefs terrible, though quite as high. Thefe
rocks deprived us of the fun at three
in the afternoon. About four miles below Paffau, Auftria is on the left, and
Bavaria on the right, as far as Ingelhart-
zeil, when we were fairly entered into
Auftria. Here is the cuftom-houfe with
which I had been threatened, and which
I approached with trepidation; but my
trunk was not opened, and nothing was
examined except my writing box, which
the officers would have unlocked. A
feal was, however, fet on my trunk,
which

which I hoped would have enabled me to pafs on to Vienna, without further plague, and then I expected to pay for all.

Thus far the Danube runs between two high mountains, and fometimes it is fo compreffed and fhut up, as to be narrower than the Thames at Mortlake. The defcent is often fo confiderable, that the water cannot be feen at the diftance of a quarter of a mile, and fometimes the noife againft rocks is as violent, and as loud as a cataract.

At the entrance into Auftria the value of money is lowered; fo that a filver piece, worth twelve *creuzers*, in Bavaria, is inftantly lowered to ten; a florin, of fixty creuzers, becomes only worth fifty; a ducat of five florins, is lowered to four florins, twelve creuzers; and a fovereign of fifteen florins, to twelve florins thirty creuzers; a louis d'or, from eleven to nine florins, twelve creuzers; and a great crown to two florins.

We went upwards of eight leagues, between

between two mountains, and ſtopt for the
night, at a wretched place, which afforded no kind of refreſhment; though I had
indulged the hope of ſupplying myſelf
here for two days to come, which being
Friday and Saturday, among Auſtrian
catholics, I knew would be kept ſtrictly
maigre.

I had now filled up the chinks of my
cabin with ſplinters, and with hay; got a
new button to the door, reconciled myſelf to my filthy blanket, and made a
pair of ſnuffers out of a chip of deal; but
alas! the eſſential failed: this was all
external, and I wanted internal comfort!
the laſt bit of my cold meat was fly-
blown, to ſuch a degree, that, ravenous
as I was, I threw it into the Danube;
bread too, that ſtaff was broken! and
nothing but Pompernickl was to be
had here; which is ſo black and ſour, as
to diſguſt two ſenſes at a time.

Friday morning, Auguſt 28th. This
river continues running through the ſame
woody,

woody, wild, and romantic country; which, to pafs through, is pleafant and entertaining, to a ftranger, but produces nothing, except firing, to the poor inhabitants. For fifty miles not a corn field or pafture is to be feen. Sheep, oxen, calves, and pigs, are all utter ftrangers in this land. I afked what was behind thefe mountains, and was anfwered, huge forefts. At Afha the country opens a little.

What an aggregate of waters is here! river after river, comes tumbling into the Danube, and yet it grows rather more deep than wide, by thefe acceffions; but many fmall rivers detach themfelves from it, and iflands are frequently formed in the middle and fides of this world of waters: before we arrived at Lintz, however, a flat fenny country appeared, with high mountains, covered with trees, at a diftance.

LINTZ.

L I N T Z.

The approach to this town, by water, is very beautiful. There is a road on each fide the Danube, at the foot of high mountains and rocks, covered with trees, by which the river is again bounded. The caſtle is feen at a diſtance, and houſes and convents, upon the ſummit of ſome of the higheſt hills, have a fine appearance. There is a bridge over the Danube of twenty very wide arches. The town is built on the ſummit and fides of high hills, and in ſituation much reſembles Paſſau. The churches were ſhut up, as it was twelve o'clock when we arrived; however, I obtained permiſſion to enter the collegiate church, where I found a large organ.

There is ſuch an appearance of piety here, as I never ſaw before in the moſt bigoted catholic countries. All along the Danube, near any town, there are little

little chapels erected, at only twenty or
thirty yards diftance from each other,
fometimes on the fides of thefe mountains, and in places too narrow for a
foot-path *; and I faw not a houfe in
Lintz that had not a Virgin or a faint,
painted or carved, upon it.

I walked about the town for near two
hours. It was market day, though but
for poor ftuff; as nothing eatable appeared, perhaps, becaufe it was Friday, but
𝕭𝖗𝖔𝖉, vile cheefe, bad apples, pears, and
plums; and of other wares, only tape,
toys, ordinary Miffals, and wretched
prints of virgins and faints. I faw not
a good fhop in the town, though there
are many fhowy and fine houfes. Gable
ends and pear-topt fteeples, in the Ba-
varian ftyle, are ftill in fafhion here.

At SPIEBURG, which is only the fhell
of an old caftle, upon a little ifland, is
the firft of the two water-falls in the Da-

---

* Thefe chapels are not fufficiently fpacious to
contain either perfons or prieft, they are only intended as receptacles for a crucifix or a Virgin.

nube,

nube, said to be so dangerous; however, now, there was nothing formidable in it but the noise.

Ens, a large city, is here in sight, upon the right hand; we went through an ugly country till it was dark; the river is sometimes like a sea, so wide that there is scarce any land in sight; at other times it is broken, and divided into small streams, by islands. The raft stopt at a hovel, on the left bank of the river, where the passengers landed, and spent the night. I remained in my cabin, where, I believe, I was much better off, as to bed, than any of them; but, for provisions, we were all on a footing. Pierre, with great difficulty, clambered up the rocks, to a village, and procured me half a dozen eggs, with which he returned in triumph. But, alas! two of them were addled, and a third had a chicken in it; which, being fast day, I could not in conscience eat.

I   Saturday,

Saturday, we fet off at five o'clock, but were ftopt, after having gone three or four miles, by a violent fog, which rendered the navigation dangerous, among fo many rocks, fhoals, and iflands. When this was difpelled, we foon reached STRU- DEL, which is fituated in a wilder country than ever I faw in paffing the Alps. Here is the famous water-fall and whirlpool, which the Germans fo much dread, that they fay it is the habitation of ꝺer Teufel; however, they had talked fo much about it, that it appeared to me lefs formidable than I expeded. The fhooting London bridge is worfe, though not attended with more noife. The company prayed and croffed themfelves moft devoutly; but though it may, efpecially in winter, be a very dangerous pafs in a boat, this raft may dip into the water, but it covers fuch a furface, that it cannot poffibly either fink or be overfet.

At IPS, a pretty town, with a new, handfome, and large *caferne,* or barrack,

O 2   juft

juſt by it, the country opens, and is very
beautiful.   Hereabouts they begin to
make Auſtrian wine : the white wine is
à pretty, pleaſant ſort, but ſmall.

At MELK, on the right of the Danube,
is a moſt magnificent convent of Bene-
dictines ; it ſeems to cover two thirds of
the town ; the architecture is beautiful,
and it has the appearance of being but
lately built : here are vines all along the
ſhore, on the left hand.   Harveſt was
quite got in hereabouts ; indeed there
is but little appearance of agriculture
in this wild country.   I believe I remarked before, that the quantity of uſeleſs woods and foreſts, in ſeveral parts of
Germany, indicate a barbarous and ſavage
people ; and, to ſay the truth, except in
the great trading towns, or thoſe where ſovereign princes reſide, the Germans ſeem
very rude and uncultivated.

The country becomes more and more
wild, as far as STEIN.   The rocks were
often ſo high, on each ſide, as to prevent

us

us from feeing the fun at two or three o'clock in the afternoon. At Stein there is a wooden bridge of twenty-five or twenty-fix very wide arches, which leads to KREMS, where the Jefuits have a moft fumptuous college, beautifully fituated on a hill; it has more the appearance of a royal palace, than any thing that we can boaft of in England. Stein is on the left, and Krems on the right hand of the Danube, going down. Here our float anchored for the night, though it was but five o'clock: indeed it had not ftopt, except early in the morning, for the fog, the whole day. We had now near fifty miles to Vienna ; and the fcoundrel Floßmeifter, or waterman, affured me, and every body at Munich, that we fhould certainly be there on Saturday night.

At Krems there is an immenfe organ, in the Jefuits' church. Here, and all the way to Vienna, the common people, in the public houfes, and the labourers, at their work, divert themfelves with fing-

ing

ing in two, and sometimes more parts.
Near Ips there was a great number of
Bohemian women, whom we should call
gypsies, on a pilgrimage to St. Mary *Tafel*, a church placed on the summit of a
very high mountain, facing the town of
Ips, on the other side the Danube. No
one could inform me why it was called
St. Mary *Tafel*; but, in all probability,
it had this appellation from the form of
the mountain on which it is placed,
which resembles a *table*. These women,
however, did not sing in parts, like the
Austrians, but in *canto fermo*, like the
pilgrims that I heard in Italy, who were
going to Assisi; the sound was carried
several miles, by the stream and wind,
down the river, upon whose smooth sur-
face it passed, without interruption.

The musical events of this week are so
trivial, as scarce to deserve recording. I
must, however, add, to what I have already said, concerning the turn for music
which I found among the Austrians, that

at

at Stein, oppofite Krems, I heard feveral
fongs and hymns, fung very well, in four
parts; who were the fingers I could not
learn, as I was on the water; but it was
a fortunate circumftance for me to be
placed, by accident, where I heard as
good a performance as could have been
procured by premeditation and defign;
it was a woman who fung the upper
part, and the melody was not only expreffed with fimplicity, but the harmony
had all the advantages of being fwelled
and diminifhed, which, to me, had the
effect of advancing and retreating; and
the performers feemed to underftand each
other, and what they were about, fo well,
that each chord had that kind of equa-
lity, in all its parts, which is given to
the fame number of notes, when played
upon the fwell of an organ. At this
place the foldiers, and almoft all the
young people that were walking by the
water fide, were frequently finging, and
never in lefs than two parts.

O 4   It

It is not eafy to account for this facility of finging in different parts, in the people of one country, more than in thofe of another : whether it arifes in Roman catholic countries, from the frequency of hearing mufic fung in parts, in their churches, I cannot fay; but of this I am certain, that in England it cofts infinite trouble, both to the mafter and fcholar, before a young practitioner in finging is able to perform, with firmnefs, an under part to the moft fimple melody imaginable; and I never remember hearing the ballad fingers, in the ftreets of London, or in our country towns, attempt finging in two different parts.

Sunday, Auguft 30. This day was trifled away without getting to Vienna with the float, as I had been fully made to expect : an officer on board, tried with me to procure a land carriage for that purpofe, but in vain. As we approached Vienna, the country became lefs favage. There are vineyards on the fides of
all

all the hills, and large iflands innumerable which divide the Danube.

Tuln is a little fortified town, with a
fine church, and a *fine* convent, which,
with a *fine* cuftom-houfe, ufually confti-
tute all the *finery* of Auftria.

At Kor Neuburg, there is a very
ftrong citadel, on the fummit of an
extreme high hill, which commands the
river and city.

At Nusdorf, a village within three
miles of Vienna, with nothing in it but
a church and a cuftom-houfe, I was quite
out of patience, at being told, that the
float could not, as it was Sunday, on any
account, enter Vienna. It was now but
five o'clock, and the feventh day of my
being immured in a fty, where, indeed
I might have grown fat if I had had any
thing to eat; but that not being the cafe,
hunger as well as lofs of time, made me
very impatient to be releafed; and after
an hour loft in trying to procure a chaife,

7 I at

I at laſt got a miſerable boat to carry me
and my ſervant to Vienna.

This voyage added but little to my
knowledge of German muſic, but a
great deal to that of the people, and
country through which I paſſed : indeed
I had an opportunity of landing at every
conſiderable town in the paſſage, where
I viſited the churches, though I had not
time to make acquaintance with muſical
people, or to collect hiſtorical materials;
but as to *national muſic*, perhaps the rude
ſongs which I heard ſung by the boors and
watermen, gave me a more genuine idea of
it, than is to be acquired from the cor-
rupted, motley, and Italianiſed melody,
to be heard in the capitals of this ex-
tenſive country.

VIENNA.

This city, the capital of the empire,
and reſidence of the imperial family, is
ſo remote from England, has been ſo
imper-

imperfectly defcribed, by writers of tra-.
vels, and is fo feldom vifited by Englifhmen, that I fhould have prefented my
readers with a minute account of its
public buildings and curiofities, if it had
not furnifhed me with ample materials
for a long article, relative to my principal fubject, MUSIC, to which every other
muft give place. I fhall, however, bef-
tow a few words on its peculiarities, and
then proceed to my mufical journal.

The approach to Vienna from the
river, is not very unlike that of Venice,
though there is much lefs water, for the
Danube divides itfelf into three ftreams,
about a mile and a half above the town;
forty or fifty towers and fpires may be
feen from the water.

The cuftom-houfe did not difappoint
my expectation of its being remarkably
troublefome, particularly, in the article
of *books;* all are ftopt there, and read
more fcrupuloufly than at the inquifi-
tion of Bologna, in Italy; and mine,
which,

which, except mufic, were merely geo-
graphical and defcriptive, were detained
near a fortnight before I could recover
them ; and his excellency lord vifcount
Stormont, his majefty's ambaffador at
this court, afterwards told me, that this
was the only thing in which it was not
in his power to affift me. On entering
the town, I was informed, that if a fingle
book had been found in my *fac de nuit*,
or travelling fatchel, its whole contents
would have been forfeited.

The ftreets are rendered doubly dark
and dirty by their narrownefs, and by
the extreme height of the houfes ; but,
as thefe are chiefly of white ftone, and in
a uniform, elegant ftyle of architecture,
in which the Italian tafte prevails, as well
as in mufic, there is fomething grand
and magnificent in their appearance,
which is very ftriking ; and even many
of thofe houfes which have fhops on the
ground-floor, feem like palaces above.
Indeed the whole town and its fuburbs,

appear,

appear, at the firft glance, to be compofed of palaces, rather than of common
habitations. The churches and convents
are chiefly of Gothic architecture ; however, the Jefuits' college is an extenfive and
elegant modern building; and the church
of St. Sophia, built on the model of St.
Peter's at Rome, but upon a much
fmaller fcale, is a beautiful copy of that
ftructure in miniature ; as is the Auftin
Friars, of the chapel of Loretto.

The emperor's prerogative of having
the firft floor of almoft every houfe in
Vienna for the ufe of the officers of his
court and army, is as fingular in itfelf,
as it is inconvenient to the inhabitants.
The houfes are fo large, that a fingle
floor fuffices for moft of the firft and
largeft families in the city.

The inhabitants do not, as elfewhere,
go to the fhops to make purchafes ; but
the fhops are *brought to them*; there
was literally a fair, at the inn where I
lodged, every day. The trades-people

feem

feem to fell nothing at home, but, like hawkers and pedlars, carry their goods from houfe to houfe. A ftranger is teafed to death by thefe chapmen, who offer to fale wretched goods, ill manufactured, and ill-fafhioned. In old England, it is is true, things are very dear, but if their goodnefs be compared with thefe, they are cheap as dirt.

I muft obferve, that I have never yet found, in any country on the continent, that the trades-people, like many in England, could be trufted, without beating them down, and fixing the price of what is purchafed of them, previous to pöffeffion. In London there is little danger of being charged unreafonably for any thing that is had from a reputable fhop, though the price is not afked, when the goods are fent for, nor paid, till the bill is brought in, perhaps a year after.

A little way out of the town, there is a famous walk, or rather ride, called the

Prat;

Prat; it is an extensive wood, or open grove, with a coach-road cut through it. There is verdure on the ground, and shade from some of the largest trees that I ever saw, with frequent views of the Danube. It is the Hyde-park of Vienna, but more flat and gloomy than that of London.

The first time I went to a theatre, I was, by mistake, carried to a German tragedy, though there was a burletta performed in Italian, the same night, at another theatre, at which were the emperor and his sisters, the arch-duchesses of Austria; but my ignorance of this, at the time, contributed to fortify, in me, that accommodating principle, which seeks profit and enjoyment from the present situation, by whatever accidents thrown into it, without repining at the loss of remote pleasures, that are unattainable.

I hoped, however, that there would be singing in this piece, but was wholly dif-

difappointed; it was **ein Trauerſpiel, von Gotthold Ephraim Leſſing,** called E-milia Galotti.

I ſhould ſuppoſe this play to have been well acted; there were energy and paſſion, and many ſpeeches were much applauded; but I was ſo young at German declamation, that I could only catch a ſentence now and then. However, I made out the drift of the piece, which very much reſembles, in the cataſtrophe, that of Virginia.

A prince of Guaſtallo, formerly in love with a counteſs, named Orſina, becomes inconſtant upon ſeeing *Emilia Galotti*, the daughter of a country gentleman, who was engaged to a worthy *Graf,* or count. He meets with this lady, at maſs, on the morning, which was fixed on for her marriage with the *Graf.*

Princes et rois vont très vite en amour, ſays M. de Voltaire. This prince has among his courtiers, a friend and confident, named Marinelli, who is a more hateful

hateful character, than Jago, in Shakefpeare's Othello.

This perfonage readily undertakes to
pander for his mafter; and having, in
vain, endeavoured to perfuade the be-
trothed *Graf*, to accept of a foreign appointment, he hires a banditti to attack
the carriage, in which *Emilia*, her mother, and the *Graf*, were proceeding to
a country-houfe, in order to celebrate
their marriage. The *Graf* is killed by
the affaffins, and *Emilia* is conveyed, in
a feeming friendly and hofpitable manner, to a *Chateau*, or country feat, of
the prince, near the road.

Orfina, the deferted miftrefs of the
prince, meeting with *Emilia*'s father,
infinuates, that the unhappy young lady
had confented to the plan, of her being
carried off, and to the murder of her
lover; which induces the irritated father, to receive from her a dagger, with
the barbarous defign of plunging it into
his daughter's bofom.

P   Mari-

Marinelli affumes the character of the friend and avenger of the deceafed *Graf*, and acquaints the father, that, as it had been rumoured, that a lover of *Emilia* had been the murderer, it would be expedient to have her feparated from her family, till the affair was cleared up.

The alarmed old man, defires permiffion to fee his daughter, alone; as foon as fhe is made acquainted with her danger, from the artful plan of Marinelli, fhe feizes the dagger which her father had fhewn her, with a refolution to deftroy herfelf. He, however, prevents her; but is at length prevailed upon, **to** give the fatal ftroke himfelf, ftimulated by her entreaties, and exaggerations of the danger to which fhe was expofed, from the lawlefs paffion of the prince, who enters at this inftant, with Marinelli.

The father confeffes the fact to the prince, and, with favage ferocity, afks him, whether he likes her now? Emilia has

I   but

but juft ftrength fufficient left, to vindi-
cate the act of her father before fhe ex-
pires. The old man delivers himfelf
into the hands of juftice; the mother
runs diftracted; while Marinelli, the chief
caufe of all the mifchief, receives no other
punifhment, with which the audience
is made acquainted, than to be ordered
by the prince, to get out of his fight.

Lady Mary Wortley Montague, gives
a curious defcription of the ftate of this
theatre, when fhe faw the comedy of
Amphitrion reprefented here, in the year
1716. " I could not eafily pardon, fays
" her ladyfhip, the liberty the poet has
" taken of larding his play with not only
" indecent expreffions, but fuch grofs
" words, as I don't think our mob would
" fuffer from a mountebank; befides the
" two Socias very fairly let down their
" breeches, in the direct view of the
" boxes, which were full of people of
" the firft rank, who feemed very well
" pleafed

" pleafed with their entertainment, and af-
" fured me, this was a celebrated piece *."

This ribald tafte has taken another
turn, and in tragedy feems now to ex-
hale itfelf in impious oaths and execra-
tions; for, in the piece of to-night, the
interlocutors curfe, fwear, and call
names, in a grofs and outrageous manner. I know not, perhaps, the exact
ideas annexed by the Germans to the
following expreffions, of 𝕭𝖊𝖞 𝕲𝖔𝖙𝖙;
𝕲𝖔𝖙𝖙 𝖛𝖊𝖗𝖉𝖆𝖒𝖒' 𝖎𝖍𝖓, &c. but they fhock-
ed my ears very frequently.

However, there is an original wild-
nefs in the conduct and fentiments of
this piece, which renders it very interefting. It is concluded by the prince
himfelf, with the following bold and
admirable exclamation; " Gods! is it.
" not a fufficient curfe to mankind, that
" princes fhould be men, but muft

* Letters of the right honourable lady Mary
Wortley Montague, vol. I.

" devils

" devils take the femblance of their
" friends * !"

This theatre is lofty, having five or
fix rows of boxes, twenty-four in each
row. The height makes it feem fhort,
yet, at the firſt glance, it is very ſtrik-
ing; it does not appear to have been
very lately painted, and looks dark; but
the fcenes and decorations are fplendid.
The ſtage had the appearance of being
oval, which, whether is was produced
by deception or reality, had a pleafing effect, as it correfponded with the
other end of the theatre, which was
rounded off at the corners, and gave an
elegant look to the whole.

The orcheſtra has a numerous band,
and the pieces which were played for
the overture and act-tunes, were very
well performed, and had an admirable

* Gott! Gott! — Iſt es, zum Unglücke ſo
mancher, nicht genug, daß Fürſten Menſchen
ſind: müſſen ſich auch noch Teufel in ihren Freund
verſtellen ?

effect;

effect; they were compofed by Haydn, Hoffman, and Vanhall.

The firft time I went to the cathedral of St. Stephen, I heard an excellent mafs, in the true church ftyle, very well performed; there were violins and violoncellos though it was not a feftival. The great organ at the weft end of this church has not been fit for ufe thefe forty years; there are three or four more organs of a fmaller fize in different parts of the church, which are ufed occafionally. That which I heard in the choir this morning is but a poor one, and as ufual, was much out of tune; it was played, however, in a very mafterly, though not a modern ftyle. All the refponfes in this fervice, are chanted in four parts, which is much more pleafing, efpecially where there is fo little melody, than the mere naked *canto fermo* ufed in moft other catholic churches; the treble part was fung by boys, and very well; particularly, by two of them, whofe

whofe voices, though not powerful, had been well cultivated.

I cannot proceed farther in the journal of my mufical tranfactions at Vienna, without mentioning the flattering manner in which I was received, protected, and even affifted in my enquiries there, by his excellency lord vifcount Stormont, his majefty's ambaffador extraordinary at that court; as it was to his lordfhip's influence and activity, that I owed the greateft part of my entertainment, and the information I acquired during my refidence at Vienna.

His lordfhip had been prepared for my arrival by a letter, which Mr. de Vifme had been fo kind as to write in my behalf, before I left Munich, in which he had explained the nature of my journey and purfuits; fo that I very foon obtained an audience, and he condefcended to enter heartily into my views, and to intereft him felf about them immediately on my arrival. This was a moft fortunate circumftance

for

for me, as his long refidence here, had furnifhed opportunities for his being perfectly acquainted with all fuch perfons and things as I wifhed to know; and that univerfal efteem and refpect, which a fteady, judicious, and amiable conduct had acquired him, joined to his high rank and ftation, rendered him all powerful in whatever caufe he efpoufed.

One of the firft fignal favours which his lordfhip conferred on me, was doing me the honour of prefenting me to the countefs Thun, a moft agreeable and accomplifhed lady of very high rank, who, among many other talents, poffeffes as great fkill in mufic as any perfon of diftinction I ever knew; fhe plays the harpfichord with that grace, eafe, and delicacy, which nothing but female fingers can arrive at.

Her favourite author for the inftrument, is a *dilettante*, M. le Comte de Becke. His pieces are very original, and
in

in a good tafte: they fhew the inftrument much, but his own delicacy and
feelings more. He was, unluckily for
me, in Bohemia at this time, fo that I
could not have the honour and advantage
of his converfation.

The fecond evening after my arrival,
I went to the French theatre, where I
faw a German comedy, or rather a farce
of five acts: however, I fhould not fuppofe the piece to be without merit, as the
natives feemed much pleafed with it.
This theatre is not fo high as that at
which I had been the night before, but
it is ftill better fitted up; here the beft
places feem to be in the pit, which is
divided in two parts, and all the feats
are ftuffed, and covered with red baize;
the fcenes were feldom changed during
the piece; but the principal, that is, the
fcene of longeft continuance, was flat
in front, where there were two large
folding doors, as in the French theatres,

for

for the entrance and exit of the principal characters. At each side there was an elegant projection, in the middle of which there was likewise a door, ufed chiefly by the fervants, and inferior characters. The comedy was often too grosly farcical; but there were fcenes, as well as characters, of real humour, and one or two of the *Comedie larmoyante* kind, that were truly pathetic.

Premiums are now no longer given, as heretofore, in this theatre, to actors who voluntarily fubmit to be kicked and cuff-ed, for the diverfion of the fpectators. It is but a few years fince, that bills were regularly brought in, at the end of each week; " So much for a flap on the " face;" " So much for a broken head; " and fo much for a kick on the breech," by the comic actors. But, in procefs of time, the effect of thefe wearing out, it became neceffary to augment their num-ber, and force, in order to render the

plea-

pleafure of the fpectators more exquifite;
'till the managers, unable any longer to
fupport fo intolerable an expence, totally
abolifhed the rewards for thefe heroic
fufferings.

And now, fince this *active wit* has
ceafed to be practifed, it is obferved that
the theatre is not only more feldom
crowded than formerly, but the audience
is become more difficult to pleafe. Indeed the confequences feem to have been
fo fatal, that many attribute the frequent
bankruptcies of the managers to the *infufferable* dullnefs and inactivity of the
performers *.

The orcheftra here was full as ftriking
as that of the other theatre, and the
pieces played were admirable. They
were fo full of invention, that it feemed
to be mufic of fome other world, info-

---

* In confideration of their great utility, it is
hoped that the worthy managers of our theatres do
not let " the fpurns and patient fuffcrings" of our
pantomime clowns, go unrewarded at the end of the
week.

much.

much, that hardly a paffage in this was to be traced ; and yet all was natural, and equally free from the ftiffnefs of labour, and the pedantry of hard ftudy. Whofe mufic it was I could not learn ; but both the compofition and performance, gave me exquifite pleafure *.

At the end of the play, there was a very fpirited and entertaining dance, planned by the celebrated ballet-mafter, M. Noverre, in which the four principal performers difplayed great abilities, in point of grace, activity, and precifion.

Three large boxes are taken out of the front of the firft row, for the imperial family, which goes frequently to this theatre; it was built by Charles the fixth. The emprefs queen continues in weeds, and

* The fymphonies of *Manheim*, excellent as they are, have been obferved, by perfons of refined tafte, to be *Manieree's*, and tirefome to fuch as continue there any time, being almoft all of one caft, from the writers of them giving too much into imitation.

has

has appeared in no public theatre since the death of the late emperor.

At night two of the poor scholars of this city sung, in the court of the inn where I lodged, duets in *falset*, *soprano*, and *contralto*, very well in tune, and with feeling and taste. I sent to enquire whether they were taught music at the Jesuits' college, and was answered in the affirmative. Though the number of poor scholars, at different colleges, amounts to a hundred and twenty, yet there are at present but seventeen that are taught music.

After this there was a band of these singers, who performed through the streets a kind of glees, in three and four parts: this whole country is certainly very musical. I frequently heard the soldiers upon guard, and centinels, as well as common people, sing in parts. The music school at the Jesuits' college, in every Roman catholic town, accounts in some measure for this faculty; yet
other

other caufes may be affigned, and, among
thefe, it fhould be remembered, that
there is fcarce a church or convent in
Vienna, which has not every morning
its *mafs in mufic:* that is, a great portion
of the church fervice of the day, fet in
parts, and performed with voices, accompanied by at leaft three or four violins, a tenor and bafe, befides the organ;
and as the churches here are daily crowded, this mufic, though not of the moft
exquifite kind, muft, in fome degree,
form the ear of the inhabitants. Phyfi-
cal caufes operate but little, I believe, as
to mufic. Nature diftributes her favours
pretty equally to the inhabitants of Europe; but moral caufes are frequently
very powerful in their effects. And it
feems as if *the national mufic of a country
was good or bad, in proportion to that of
its church fervice;* which may account
for the tafte of the common people of
Italy, where indeed the language is more
mufical than in any other country of
Europe,

Europe, which certainly has an effect
upon their vocal mufic; but the excellent performances that are every day
heard for nothing in the churches, by
the common people, more contribute to
refine and fix the national tafte for good
mufic, than any other thing that I can at
prefent fuggeft.

I had the good fortune to meet with
the admirable poet Metaftafio here, and
the no lefs admirable mufician Haffe, as
well as with the chevalier Gluck, one of
the moft extraordinary geniufes of this, or,
perhaps, of any age or nation; and as I was
fo happy as to enjoy the converfation of
thefe illuftrious perfonages very frequently, during my refidence in this city, it
will incline me to be very circumftantial
concerning them, which I hope my
readers will pardon in behalf of their
extraordinary merit, and the enthufiaftic
admiration of it, with which I confefs
my mind to be impreffed.

Be-

Before I had the honour of being introduced to Signor Metaſtaſio, I obtained, from undoubted authority, the following particulars relative to this great poet, whoſe writings have perhaps more contributed to the refinement of vocal melody, and, conſequently, of muſic in general, than the joint efforts of all the great compoſers in Europe; this ſuppoſition I ſhall hereafter endeavour to explain and confirm, in ſpeaking of him only as a lyric poet.

The *Abate Pietro Metaſtaſio*, was adopted at Rome, while very young, by the celebrated civilian, Gravina, who diſcovering in him an extraordinary talent for poetry, undertook the care of his education; and, after he had been inſtructed under his eye, in all the parts of polite literature, he ſent him to Calabria, in the kingdom of Naples, to learn Greek, as a living language, it being ſtill ſpoken in that province, by the natives. He

had

had such a faculty of speaking verses extempore, so early as at five years old, that
Gravina used to set him on a table, to
perform the part of an *Improvvisatore* ;
but this exercise was found to exhaust
him so much, that a physician assured
his patron, if he continued the practice, it would destroy him ; for at such
times he was so truly *afflatus numine,*
that his head and stomach swelled, and
became inflamed, while his extremities
grew cold. Gravina seeing this, thought
it necessary to take the physician's advice, and would never suffer him more
to *improvvisare.* Metastasio now speaks of
the practice as equally repugnant to
grammar, and to common sense ; for
whoever accustoms himself in this rapid
manner, to distort every thought into
rhyme, destroys all taste, and totally pre-
cludes selection : till, by degrees, the mind
and genius accommodating themselves to
inaccuracies and absurdities, not only

Q   lose

lofe a relifh for labour, but for every
thing that is chafte and correct.

Gravina made Metaftafio tranflate all
Homer into Italian verfe, before he was
fourteen years of age ; and this, perhaps,
deftroyed fome of that veneration for the
ancients, with which moft men of true
genius are poffeffed *. Fielding faid of
himfelf, that he bore *marks* of the difficulty
of Homer about him all his life. Gravina idolized the ancients, and, perhaps,
Metaftafio, taking the *contrepied,* refpects
them too little.

He has opinions fixed and unalterable,
peculiar to himfelf, concerning many
things, particularly rhyme: he ftill thinks
that the Hebrew Pfalms are in rhyme,
and that this confonance of verfes is infinitely more ancient than is generally imagined. He thinks that Milton's Paradife
Loft cannot be a perfect poem becaufe
it is written in *blank verfe,* though all

* Gravina died in the year 1718, and made Metaftafio his heir.

the

the narrative parts of his own dramatic pieces are in meafured profe; indeed, before each fong, he has a couplet, or clofe, ufually in rhyme, which prepares for the change.

The whole tenor of his life is equally innoxious with his writings. He lives with the moft mechanical regularity, which he fuffers none to difturb; he has not dined from home thefe thirty years; he is very difficult of accefs, and equally averfe to new perfons, and new things; he fees, in a familiar way, but three or four people, and them, conftantly every night, from eight o'clock till ten; he ab- hors writing, and never fets pen to paper but by compulfion: as it was neceffary to bind Silenus, before he would fing; and Proteus, to oblige him to give oracles.

He has long been invefted with the title and appointments of imperial lau- reate; and when the emperor, emprefs, or any one of the imperial family orders it, he fits down and writes, two hours

at

at a time only, juft as he would tran-
fcribe a poem written by any one elfe;
never waiting for a call, invoking the
Mufe, or even receiving her favours at
any other than his own ftated periods.

He was applied to by the editors of
the *Encyclopedie,* to write the article
Opera for that work; but he politely
declined the tafk, fuppofing it impoffible
that his fentiments on the fubject fhould
be pleafing to the French nation.

Taffo is his favourite of all poets; he
likes not Fingal, on account of its wild-
nefs and obfcurity *; he reads with his
felect friends ancient and modern authors
every evening; he is extremely fond
of the writings of count Medini, a Bohemian, whofe poetical compofitions,
he fays, are fuperior to thofe of all other
living writers. This count is tranflating

---

* The poems of Offian are tranflated into Italian, by the Abate Melchior Cefarotti, and were
publifhed at Padua in 1763.

the *Henriade*, of Voltaire, into Italian *Ottave Rime*.

A perfon of very high rank affured me, that he had been five years in Vienna before he could get acquainted with Me-taftafio, or even into converfation with him; and, after that time, but three vifits had been exchanged between them in feveral years; indeed, in my applications for letters of recommendation to this exquifite poet, before I left England, I had been mortified by an affurance, " that " it would be in vain for me to attempt " even a fight of Metaftafio, as he was " totally worn out, incommunicative, " and averfe to fociety on all occafions."

However, this account had been ex-preffed in too ftrong terms; for, upon my arrival at Vienna, I found that be-fides the conftant fociety of his particular friends every evening, he had a kind of levee each morning, at which he was vifited by a great number of perfons of high rank and diftinguifhed merit.

Q 3　　　　If

If he is attended to with complaifance, he converfes very freely and agreeably; but if contradicted, he becomes immediately filent; he is too well-bred, as well as too indolent, to difpute; if what he thinks erroneous be advanced, in oppofition to any thing that he has faid, he paffes it over in filence. He likes not animated difcuffions, fuch as generally fubfift among men of talents and learning; but rather chufes the eafe and moderation of a private individual, than to lay down the law in the decifive manner of a public and exalted character. Indeed there feems to be that foft calmnefs in his life, which fubfifts in his writings, where he reafons, even in paffion, more than he raves; and that even tenor of propriety and correctnefs which runs through all his works, is, in fome degree, conftitutional. He is as feldom, perhaps, violently agitated in his writings as in his life, and he may be called the poet of the golden age; in which fim-

plicity

plicity and decorum are faid to have reigned, more than the wild and furious paffions. The effufions of patriotifm, love, and friendfhip, which he pours out with exquifite fweetnefs, are affections of a foft and gentle kind, which his heart felt, and his foul has coloured.

He has not, perhaps, the fire of a Corneille, or the wit and variety of a Voltaire; but he has all the pathos, all the correctnefs of a Racine, with more originality. I need only mention his well-known poem, *Grazie a gl'Inganni tuoi*, which has been fo many times imitated and tranflated in all languages: this contains a fpecies of wit, peculiar to Metaftafio, in which he turns trivial circumftances to account. Shakefpeare has faid, in derifion, of one of his characters, that " he has a *reafonable* good wit," and this is ferioufly true with refpect to Metaftafio, whofe wit is not compofed of epigrammatic points, or whimfical conceits; neither is it biting nor farcaftical;

Q 4   but

but confifts of familiar and natural things,
highly polifhed, and fet in diamonds.

> ———'Tis nature to advantage drefs'd,
> What oft was thought, but ne'er fo well ex-
> prefs'd.

The fweetnefs of his language and
verfification, give a grace to all that he
writes, and the natural tendency of his
genius, is to point out rectitude, propriety, and decorum; and though he
difcovers in every ftanza of his Nifa,
that he is not cured of his paffion for a
jilt, yet he plainly proves that he ought
to be fo.

Party runs as high among poets, muficians, and their adherents, at Vienna
as elfewhere. Metaftafio and Haffe,
may be faid, to be at the head of one of
the principal fects; and Calfabigi and
Gluck of another. The firft, regarding
all innovations as quackery, adhere to
the ancient form of the mufical drama,
in which the poet and mufician claim
equal attention from an audience; the

bard

bard in the recitatives and narrative parts;
and the compofer in the airs, duos, and
choruffes. The fecond party depend
more on theatrical effects, propriety of
character, fimplicity of diction, and of
mufical execution, than on, what *they*
ftyle, flowery defcriptions, fuperfluous
fimiles, fententious and cold morality,
on one fide, with tirefome fymphonies,
and long divifions, on the other *. It is
lefs my bufinefs and intention here, to
take fides, or to determine which of thefe
parties are right, than to point out the
different merit of both. For I fhould
not only be an enemy to my own pleafure, but unworthy of the title I have
affumed, of a faithful hiftorian, if I encouraged exclufive approbation. I fhall
therefore proceed in characterifing the

* *L'Autore a foftuito alle fiorite defcrizioni, ai Pa-
ragoni fuperflui, e alle fentenziofe e fredde moralità,
il linguaggio del cuore, le paffioni forti, le fituazioni
intereffanti, e uno fpettacolo fempre variato.* Dedicaz.
d' Alefte, dal cav. Gluck.

genius

genius of the two great compofers above-
mentioned, to the beft of my judgment
and feelings, unbiaffed by the decifions
of others.

The merit of Signor Haffe has fo long,
and fo univerfally been eftablifhed on the
continent, that I have never yet converfed with a fingle profeffor on the fubject, who has not allowed him to be
the moft natural, elegant, and judicious
compofer of vocal mufic, as well as the
moft voluminous now alive *; equally a
friend to poetry and to the voice, he
difcovers as much judgment as genius,
in expreffing words, as well as in accompanying thofe fweet and tender melodies,
which he gives to the finger. Always regarding the voice, as the firft object of
attention in a theatre, he never fuffocates
it, by the learned jargon of a multipli-
city of inftruments and fubjects; but is

* He was born at Bergendorf, in Lower Saxony, within eight miles of Hamburg, and is
beft known in Italy, by the name of *Il Saffone*.

as

as careful of preferving it's importance, as a painter, of throwing the ftrongeft light upon the capital figure of his piece.

In 1769, he produced at Vienna the mufic of a little opera, or *Intermezzo tragico, Piramo e Tifbe, à tre voci*; and in 1771, he fet *Ruggiero*, at Milan, for the marriage of the arch-duke Ferdinand, brother of the emperor, with the prin- cefs of Modena, both written by Metaf- tafio *.

Dr. Brown pretended to prove, the feparation of mufic and poetry; if he was right, it muft, however, be allowed that this poet and mufician are the *two halves* of what, like Plato's *Androgyne*, once confti- tuted a *whole*; for as they are equally pof- feffed of the fame characteriftic marks of

---

* Thefe pieces are the laft productions of the great poet and mufician, who, with more pro- priety than Pope and Jarvis, might fay,

Smit with the love of fifter arts we came,

And met congenial, mingling flame with flame.

true

true genius, tafte, and judgment; fo propriety, confiftency, clearnefs, and precifion, are alike the infeparable compa-
nions of both. When the voice was more
refpected than the fervile herd of imita-
tive inftruments, and at a time when a
different degree, and better judged kind
of ftudy rendered it, perhaps, more worthy of attention than at prefent, the airs
of Signor Haffe, particularly thofe of the
pathetic kind, were fuch as charmed every
hearer, and fixed the reputation of the firft
fingers in Europe * .

His abilities are but little known in
England, as but few of his compofitions
are printed, and thofe of the moft trivial
kind; but, as his works are more numerous than thofe of any vocal compofer
now living, he may, without injury to
his brethren, be allowed to be as fuperior to all other lyric compofers, as
Metaftafio is to all other lyric poets.

* Such as Farinelli, Fauftina, Mingotti, &c.

The

The chevalier Gluck is fimplifying mufic; and with unbounded invention and powers for creating capricious difficulties, and decking his melodies with meretricious ornaments, he tries all he can to keep his mufe chafte and fober, his three operas of *Orfeo, Alcefte,* and *Paride,* are proofs of this, as they contain few difficulties of execution, though many of expreffion.

He has lately fuggefted to an able writer, a plan for a new ode on St. Cecilia's day, which difcovers both genius and difcernment. Lord Cowper had, fome time fince, Dryden's Ode performed to Handel's mufic at Florence; but fet to a literal Italian tranflation given *totidem fyllabis,* in order to preferve the mufic as entire as poffible. But this tendernefs for the mufician, was fo much at the expence of the poet, that Dryden's divine Ode, became not only unpoetical, but unintelligible in this wretched verfion. The mufic has fince been performed at

6 Vienna

Vienna to the fame words, and many parts of it were very much liked, in defpite of the nonfenfe through which it was conveyed to the ears of the audience.

Gluck was exceedingly ftruck with the thoughts of our great poet, and wifhed to have an ode on the fame fubject, but written on a different plan, which would preferve as many of them as poffible. His idea was this; a poem of fo great a length, could never be fung to modern mufic by *one perfon*. Now, as Dryden's Ode is all *narrative*; there feems no propriety in diftributing it among different perfons, in the performance. He wifhed therefore, to have it thrown into a dramatic form, in which the interlocutors might fpeak what paffion fuggefts; and this has been done in the following manner: it begins with a feaft of Bacchus, at which Alexander and Thais prefide. They agree to call in Timotheus to fing to them; but before his arrival, the hero and his miftrefs differ in opinion con-

concerning his merit; the one fuppofes him to be inferior to what has been reported of him; and the other, fuperior. This contention enlivens the dialogue, and interefts the audience till the arrival of the bard, who begins to fing of the Trojan war, which animates Alexander fo much, that he breaks out into the complaints attributed to him by the old ftory of having no Homer, like Achilles, to record his actions.

Tuefday, September 1ft. At vefpers, this afternoon, I heard, in the cathedral, fome admirable old mufic compofed by Fux, not very well performed, indeed, as to finging or accompaniments; the former was feeble, and the latter, I mean the violins, were defpicable: however, the organ was very well played, by the organift, M. Mittermeir. M. Hoffman, an excellent compofer of inftrumental mufic, particularly of fymphonies, is *maeftro di capella*. The church is a dark, dirty, and difmal old Gothic building, though richly ornamented; in it are hung all the trophies of war, taken from the Turks and other enemies of the house of Austria, for more than a century past, which gives it very much the appearance of an old wardrobe.

At half an hour past six this evening, I went to the comic opera of *Il Barone*. The music, composed by Signor Salieri, a scholar of M. Gasman. I did not receive much pleasure from the overture, or the two first airs ; the music was languid, and the singing but indifferent. There were only four characters in the piece, and the principal woman did not appear till the third scene ; but then she gave a glow to every thing around her ; it was one of the Baglioni, of Bologna *, whom I had heard both at Milan and Florence, during my tour through Italy. She is very much improved since that time, and her voice is now one of the clearest,

* Costanza.

sweetest,

fweeteft, trueft, moft powerful, and extenfive I ever heard. In compafs, it is
from Bb, on the fifth fpace in the bafe,
to D in alt; full; fteady, and equal ; her
fhake is good; and her *Portamento* admirably free from the nofe, mouth, or
throat. There was fuch a roundnefs and
dignity in all the tones, that every thing
fhe did became interefting ; a few plain
flow notes from her, were more acceptable to the audience, than a whole elaborate air from any one elfe.

This finger is young, has good fea-
tures, the *embonpoint charmant*, and is
upon the whole a fine figure ; but I cannot attribute all the improvement I now
found in her voice to time; fomething
muft be given to the difference of theatres ; thofe of Florence and Milan, are
are at leaft twice as big as this at
Vienna, which is about the fize of our
great opera houfe; in the Hay-market.
The opera of to-night was performed in
the German theatre, where I had before

R feen

feen a tragedy. The two theatres of
Vienna are never both open together,
except on a Sunday or feftival, at other
times they are opened alternately.

The emperor, the arch-duke Maxi-
milian, his brother, and his two fifters,
the arch-ducheffes Marianne, and Mary
Elizabeth, were all at this burletta.
The box, in which they fate, was very
little diftinguifhed from the reft; they
came in and went out with few attendants, and without parade. The emperor is of a manly fine figure, and has
a fpirited and pleafing countenance; he
often changes his place at the opera, to
converfe with different perfons, and frequently walks about the ftreets without
guards, feeming to fhun, as much as poffible, all kinds of unneceffary pomp.
His imperial majefty was extremely attentive during the performance of the
opera, and applauded the Baglione feveral
times very much.

The

The admiffion into this theatre is at a
very eafy rate; twenty-four *Creuzers*
only are paid for going into the pit; in
which, however, there are feats with
backs to them. A *Creuzer* here, is
hardly equal to an Englifh halfpenny;
indeed, part of the front of the pit is
railed off, and is called the amphitheatre;
for places there, the price is doubled, none
are to be had for money, except in the
pit and the flips, which run all along
the top of the houfe, and in which only
fixteen *Creuzers* are paid. The boxes
are all let by the feafon to the principal
families, as is the cuftom in Italy.

The fize of this theatre may be nearly
imagined, by comparing with any one
of our own, the number of boxes and
feats in each. There are in this five
ranks of boxes, twenty-four in each;
in the pit there are twenty-feven rows
of feats, which feverally contain twenty-
four perfons.

Wed-

Wednefday, September 2. This morning was dedicated to the delivering of letters, with which I was furnifhed to different perfons in Vienna. Among whom, I muft diftinguifh two, from whofe acquaintance I derived great pleafure, as well as affiftance in my mufical refearches; thefe were the *abáte Taruffi, uditore e fegretario di legazione* to the pope's nuncio, to whom I was favoured with a letter from Mr. Baretti; and M. L'Augier, one of the principal phyficians to the inperial court, to the knowledge of whom I was indebted to Col. St. Pol, and M. de Vifme, who were both fo kind as to write to him in my behalf.

It afforded me fingular fatisfaction to converfe with the *abate Taruffi,* as I found him to have not only a general knowledge of every fubject that was ftarted, but poffeffed of a fuperior tafte in literature and the arts; he fpeaks Englifh, and is fo perfectly acquainted with the writings

of

of our beſt authors, both in verſe and
proſe, that he quotes them as readily
and happily as a native of Great Britain.

During my firſt viſit I made him acquainted with the particular object of my
journey into Germany, and furniſhed
him with the printed account of my tour
through France and Italy. I was happy
to find that he was a particular acquaintance of Metaſtaſio and of Haſſe, and the
more ſo as he voluntarily offered to introduce me to both. He likewiſe promiſed
to preſent me to the legate, and to the
Duca di Breſciano, not only as to perſons whoſe influence might be of uſe to
me, from their high rank, but whoſe
converſation, from their knowledge and
love of muſic, might furniſh both anecdotes and reflections well worth my attention. He favoured me with ſeveral inte-
reſting particulars relative to Metaſtaſio,
one of which was, that a young lady, the
daughter of a deceaſed friend, who was
born, educated, and who ſtill lived in the

R 3   ſame

fame houfe with him, had the greateft genius for mufic, in all its branches of playing, finging, and compofing, of any one living. Metaftafio, at firft, inftructed her, how to fet his fongs; but now fhe delights and even aftonifhes the great poet himfelf.

I was extremely curious to know what kind of mufic would beft fulfil the ideas of Metaftafio, when applied to his own poetry; and imagined that this young lady, with all the advantages of his inftructions, counfel, and approbation, combined with her own genius, muft be an *alter idem*, and that her productions would include every mufical embellifhment which could be fuperadded to his poetry, without deftroying or diminifhing its native beauty. Lord Stormont had kindly undertaken to bring about an interview, between Metaftafio and me; fo that till this had taken place, I was not at liberty to vifit him with Signor Taruffi; however, he promifed immediately

ately to read my book, and to apprize him of its contents, in order to prepare him for my acquaintance.

M. L'Augier, in defpight of uncom‑ mon corpulency, poffeffes a moft active and cultivated mind. His houfe is the rendezvous of the firft people of Vienna, both for rank and genius; and his con‑ verfation is as entertaining, as his knowledge is extenfive and profound. Among his other acquirements he has ar‑ rived at great fkill in mufic, has a moft refined and diftiguifhing tafte, and has heard *national melody* in all parts of the world with philofophical ears.

He has been in France, Spain, Portu‑ gal, Italy, and Conftantinople, and is, in fhort, a living hiftory of modern mufic. In Spain he was intimately acquainted with Domenico Scarlatti, who, at feven‑ ty‑three, compofed for him a great num‑ ber of harpfichord leffons which he now poffeffes, and of which he favoured me with copies. The book in which they

R 4   are

are tranfcribed, contains forty-two pieces, among which are feveral flow movements, and of all thefe, I, who have been a collector of Scarlatti's compofitions all my life, had never feen more than three or four. They were compofed in 1756, when Scarlatti was too fat to crofs his hands as he ufed to do, fo that thefe are not fo difficult, as his more juvenile works, which were made for his fcholar and patronefs, the late queen of Spain, when princefs of Afturias.

Scarlatti frequently told M. L'Augier, that he was fenfible he had broke through all the rules of compofition in his leffons; but afked if his deviations from thefe rules offended the ear? and, upon being anſwered in the negative, he faid, that he thought there was fcarce any other rule, worth the attention of a man of genius, than that of not difpleafing the only fenfe of which mufic is the object*,

* Scarlatti was the firſt who dared to give way to fancy in his compofitions, by breaking through

There

There are many paſſages in Scarlatti's pieces, in which he imitated the melody of tunes ſung by carriers, muleteers, and common people. He uſed to ſay, that the muſic of Alberti, and of ſeveral other modern compoſers, did not, in the execution, want a harpſichord, as it might be equally well, or perhaps, better ex-preſſed by any other inſtrument; but, as nature had given him ten fingers, and, as his inſtrument had employment for them all, he ſaw no reaſon why he ſhould not uſe them.

M. L'Augier ſung to me ſeveral frag-ments of Bohemian, Spaniſh, Portugueſe, and Turkiſh muſic, in which the peculiar expreſſion depended on the *contre tems,* or breach of ſtrict time; beat the mea-

the contracted prohibitions of rules drawn from dull compoſitions produced in the infancy of the art, and which ſeemed calculated merely to keep it ſtill in that ſtate. Before his time, the *eye* was made the ſovereign judge of muſic, but Scarlatti ſwore allegiance only to the *ear.*

ſure,

sure, and keep it as exactly as is neceffary, in more refined and modern mufic,
and it wholly lofes its effect *.

He furnifhed me with an anecdote
concerning Caffarelli and Gizziello, fimilar to that which I have given in my
former journal, relative to Senefino and
Farinelli.

When Gizziello firft fung at Rome,
his performance fo far enchanted every
hearer, that it became the general fubject of converfation, which not only
contributed to fpread his fame through
that city, but to extend it to the moft
remote parts of Italy; it is natural to
fuppofe that the account of this new mufical phenomenon foon reached Naples,
and equally natural to imagine that it

* It has been fuppofed, that the ancient Greeks
had fcales of founds, in which the *intervals* were
divided into more minute parts, than any that are
to be found in modern mufic; and it feems, as if
our prefent divifions of *time*, were far from in-
cluding every variety of meafure poffible.

I   was

was not heard with indifference in a place where fo powerful a propenfity to mu-fical pleafure prevails. Caffarelli, at this time in the zenith of his reputation, was fo · far piqued by curiofity, perhaps by jealoufy, that he took an opportunity, the firft time he could be fpared from the opera at Naples, to ride poft all night, in order to hear that at Rome. He enter-ed the pit, muffled up in a *pellice*, or fur-gown, unknown by any one there; and, after he had heard Gizziello fing a fong, he cried out, as loud as he poffibly could, *bravo! braviffimo! Gizziello, è Caffarelli che ti lo dice,* 'tis Caffarelli who applauds—and, immediately quitting the theatre, he fet out on his return to Naples the fame night.

M. L'Augier told me that the emprefs queen had been a notable mufician. Some years ago he had heard her fing very well; and in the year 1739, when fhe was only twenty-two years of age, and very handfome, fhe fung a *duo* with Senefino, at Florence, fo well, that, by

her

her voice, which was then a very fine one, and graceful and steady manner, she so captivated the old man, Senesino, that he could not proceed without shedding tears of satisfaction. Her imperial majesty has so long been a performer, that, the other day, in pleasantry, she told the old Fauftina, the wife of Haffe, who is still living, and upwards of seventy years of age, that she thought herself the first, meaning the oldeft, *virtuofa* in Europe; for her father brought her on the court stage, at Vienna, when she was only five years old, and made her sing a song.

The whole imperial family is musical; the emperor perhaps juft enough for a sovereign prince, that is, with sufficient hand, both on the violoncello and harpsichord, to amuse himself, and sufficient taste and judgment to hear, understand, and receive delight from others. A person of great distinction told me, that he saw, some years ago, four arch-duchesses

of

of Auftria, the emperor's fifters, app'ear
at court in the opera of *Egeria*, written
by Metaftafio, and fet by Haffe, exprefsly
for their ufe. They were then extremely beautiful, fung and acted very well,
for princeffes, and the grand duke of
Tufcany, who was likewife very handfome, danced, in the character of Cupid.

I found that M. L'Augier had himfelf
been a good harpfichord player: he now
reads and judges of mufic very accurately.
During my firft vifit, he was fo obliging
as to promife to make me acquainted
with Haffe, Gluck, Wagenfeil, Haydn,
and all the muficians that were worth
my attention, in Vienna; and fixed on
the next evening for giving me an opportunity of hearing fome of Haydn's
quartettos, performed with the utmoft
precifion and perfection, as well as a
little girl, of eight or nine years old, who
is regarded here as a prodigy, on the
harpfichord.

I had

I had the honour of dining to-day with his excellency lord Stormont, who had been fo kindly attentive, as to invite a mufical party to meet me; among whom were prince Poniatowfki, brother to the king of Poland, a great lover of mufic, and the count and countefs Thun. The countefs, who interefts herfelf very much in every thing that concerns mufic, and who reads and fpeaks Englifh, honoured my Account of the Prefent State of Italian Mufic with an attentive perufal, as lord Stormont had done before : this enabled them to judge of my mufical wants better than I could have done in converfation, without bearing too large a fhare in it.

Countefs Thun has nothing about her that reminds one of the pride or heavinefs attributed by travellers to the Germans : on the contrary, fhe is naturally and innocently chearful and humorous : has fallies of wit, and excites mirth by a

pleafant

pleafant irony, peculiar to herfelf. She had been fo kind as to write a note to Gluck on my account, and he had returned, for *him*, a very civil anfwer; for he is as formidable a character as Handel ufed to be: a very dragon, of whom all are in fear. However, he had agreed to be vifited in the afternoon; and lord Stormont and countefs Thun had extended their condefcenfion fo far as to promife to carry me to him.

But before we fet out, the duke of Braganza, and much other company, came in; lord Stormont did me the honour to prefent me to his highnefs, who is an excellent judge of mufic, and who condefcended to converfe with me a confiderable time on the fubject. This prince is a great traveller, having vifited England, France, and Italy, before his arrival in Germany. He is very lively, and occafioned much mirth by his pleafantries, which were all feafoned with *good humour*.

His

His royal highness gave me an account
of a Portuguese Abbé, whom lord Stormont and M. Laugier had before mentioned as a person of a very singular
character; a kind of Rousseau, but still
more original. He is of the most difficult access; refuses every offer of service
in the way of money and presents, though
he has nothing but his mass to subsist
on, which produces him just fifteen pence
a day. He is determined to be indepen-
dent, and hates to be talked of by the
world, and almost to talk to any one in
it. The duke of Braganza, however,
thought he had just interest sufficient to
make him and me acquainted; and as
another select musical party was forming
on my account, for Friday, to dine with
lord Stormont, the duke promised to do
all in his power to bring this extraordinary Abate with him. His musical
opinions are as singular as his character.
He plays very well on the large Spanish
guittar, though in a very peculiar style:
with

with little melody, but, with refpect to harmony and modulation, in the moft pleafing and original manner.

He is a profeffed enemy to the fyftem of Rameau, and thinks the *Baffe Fonda-mentale* the moft abfurd of all inventions; as it deftroys all fancy, connection, and continuity, by perpetually tending to a *final clofe* and termination of whatever is begun: falling a fifth, or rifing a fourth, cuts every thing off fhort, or makes the ear, which is accuftomed to a fundamental bafe, uneafy till a paffage is finifhed.

At five o'clock lord Stormont's coach carried madame Thun, his lordfhip, and myfelf, to the houfe of the chevalier Gluck, in the Fauxbourg St. Mark. He is very well houfed there; has a pretty garden, and a great number of neat, and elegantly furnifhed rooms. He has no children; madame Gluck, and his niece, who lives with him, came to receive us at the door, as well as the ve-

S   teran

teran compofer himfelf. He is much
pitted with the fmall-pox, and very
coarfe in figure and look, but was foon
got into good humour; and he talked,
fung, and played, madame Thun obferved, more than ever fhe knew him at
any one time.

He began, upon a very bad harpfichord, by accompanying his niece, who
is but thirteen years old, in two of the
capital fcenes of his own famous opera
of *Alcefte*. She has a powerful and well-
toned voice, and fung with infinite tafte,
feeling, expreffion, and even execution.
After thefe two fcenes from *Alcefte*, fhe
fung feveral others, by different compofers, and in different ftyles, particularly
by Traetta.

I was affured that mademoifelle Gluck
had learned to fing but two years, which,
confidering the perfection of her performance, really aftonifhed me. She began finging under her uncle, but he, in
a precipitate fit of defpair, had given her

up;

up; when Signor Millico, arriving at
Vienna about the fame time, and difco-
vering that fhe had an improvable voice,
and a docile difpofition, begged he might
be allowed to teach her for a few months
only, in order to try whether it would
not be worth her while ftill to perfevere
in her mufical ftudies, notwithftanding
the late decifion againft her; which he
fufpected had its rife from the impatience
and impetuofity of the uncle, more than
the want of genius in the niece. Her
performance now is an equal proof of the
fagacity and penetration of Signor Millico, in making this difcovery, and of
the excellent method with which he
conveys his inftructions; for this young
lady has fo well caught his tafte and expreffion, and made them fo much her
own, that they have none of the cold-
nefs of imitation, but feem wholly derived from her own feelings; and it is a
ftyle of finging, perhaps, ftill more irre-
fiftibly grateful and enchanting in a fe-

male,

male, than even in Signor Millico himfelf.

Mademoifelle Gluck is thin, feems
of a delicate conftitution, and, as fhe
fings fo much in earneft, I fhould fear
for her health if fhe were to make
finging a profeffion; but fhe is not intended for a public performer.

When fhe had done, her uncle was
prevailed upon to fing himfelf; and, with
as little voice as poffible, he contrived to
entertain, and even delight the company,
in a very high degree; for, with the
richnefs of accompaniment, the energy
and vehemence of his manner in the *Al-
legros*, and his judicious expreffion in
the flow movements, he fo well com-
penfated for the want of voice, that it
was a defect which was foon entirely for-
gotten.

He was fo good-humoured as to perform almoft his whole opera of *Alcefte*;
many admirable things in a ftill later
opera of his, called *Paride ed Elena*; and in
a French

a French opera, from Racine's *Iphigenie*,
which he has juft compofed. This
laft, though he had not as yet committed
a note of it to paper, was fo well digefted
in his head, and his retention is fo wonderful, that he fung it nearly from the
beginning to the end, with as much rea-
dinefs as if he had had a fair fcore before
him.

His invention is, I believe, unequalled
by any other compofer who now lives,
or has ever exifted, particularly in dramatic painting, and theatrical effects.
He ftudies a poem a long time before he
thinks of fetting it. He confiders well
the relation which each part bears to
the whole; the general caft of each
character, and afpires more at fatisfying
the mind, than flattering the ear. This
is not only being a friend to poetry, but
a poet himfelf; and if he had language
fufficient, of any other kind than that
of found, in which to exprefs his ideas, I
am certain he would be a great poet; as

it

it is, mufic, in his hands, is a moſt co-
pious, nervous, elegant, and expreſſive
language.   It ſeldom happens that a
ſingle air of his operas can be taken out
of its niche, and ſung ſingly, with much
effect; the whole is a chain, of which a
detached ſingle link is but of ſmall importance.

If it be poſſible for the partizans of
old French muſic to hear any other than
that of Lulli and Rameau, with pleaſure,
it muſt be M. Gluck's *Iphigenie*, in which
he has ſo far accommodated himſelf to
the national taſte, ſtyle, and language, as
frequently to imitate and adopt them,
The chief obſtacles to his fame, perhaps,
among his contracted judges, but which
will be moſt acceptable to others, is that
there is frequently *melody*, and always
meaſure, in his muſic, though ſet to
French words, and for a *ſerious French
opera.*

I reminded M. Gluck of his air, *Raſſe-
rena il Meſto Ciglio,* which was in ſuch
great

great favour in England, fo long ago as
the year 1745 ; and prevailed upon him,
not only to fing that, but feveral others
of his firft and moft favourite airs. He
told me that he owed entirely to England the ftudy of nature in his dramatic
compofitions : he went thither at a very
difadvantageous period ; Handel was then
fo high in fame, that no one would will-
ingly liften to any other than to his
compofitions. The rebellion broke out;
all foreigners were regarded as dangerous
to the ftate; the opera-houfe was fhut
up, by order of the Lord Chamberlain,
and it was with great difficulty and addrefs that lord Middlefex obtained permiffion to open it again, with a temporary
and political performance, *La Caduta de
Giganti.* This *Gluck* worked upon with
fear and trembling, not only on account of
the few friends he had in England, but
from an apprehenfion of riot and popular fury, at the opening of the theatre,
in which none but foreigners and papifts
were employed.

S 4   He

He then ſtudied the Engliſh taſte; remarked particularly what the audience ſeemed moſt to feel; and finding that plainneſs and ſimplicity had the greateſt effect upon them, he has, ever ſince that time, endeavoured to write for the voice, more in the natural tones of the human affections and paſſions, than to flatter the lovers of deep ſcience or difficult execution; and it may be remarked, that moſt of his airs in *Orfeo* are as plain and ſimple as Engliſh ballads; and the additions that were made to it when firſt performed in England, by Meſſrs. Bach and Guglielmi, were of ſo different a texture, though excellent in another way, that they deſtroyed the *unity* of ſtyle and characteriſtic ſimplicity, for which, when performed at Vienna, this production was ſo much admired.

M. Gluck has developed his ideas of the neceſſary requiſites of dramatic muſic ſo fully, in his dedication of *Alceſte*, to the grand duke of Tuſcany; and has given his reaſons for deviating from the

beaten

beaten track, with so much force and freedom, that I shall make no apology for presenting my readers, with an extract from it.

"When I undertook to set this poem, "it was my design to divest the "music entirely of all those abuses "with which the vanity of singers, or "the too great complacency of compo- "sers, has so long disfigured the Italian "opera, and rendered the most beauti- "ful and magnificent of all public ex- "hibitions, the most tiresome and ridi- "culous. It was my intention to "confine music to its true dramatic pro- "vince, of assisting poetical expression, "and of augmenting the interest of the "fable; without interrupting the action, "or chilling it with useless and super- "fluous ornaments; for the office of "music, when joined to poetry, seemed "to me, to resemble that of colouring "in a correct and well disposed design, "where the lights and shades only seem
"to

" to animate the figures, without altering
" the out-line.

" I determined therefore not to ſtop
" an actor, in the heat of a ſpirited dia-
" logue, for a tedious *ritornel*; nor to
" impede the progreſs of paſſion, by
" lengthening a ſingle ſyllable of a fa-
" vourite word, merely to diſplay agility
" of throat; and I was equally inflexible
" in my reſolution, not to employ the
" orcheſtra to ſo poor a purpoſe, as that
" of giving time for the recovery of
" breath, ſufficient for a long and un-
" meaning cadence.

" I never thought it neceſſary to hurry
" through the ſecond part of a ſong,
" though the moſt impaſſioned and im-
" portant, in order to repeat the words
" of the firſt part, regularly four times,
" merely to finiſh the air, where the
" ſenſe is unfiniſhed, and to give an op-
" portunity to the ſinger, of ſhewing
" that he has the impertinent power
" of varying paſſages, and diſguiſing
" them,

" them, till they shall be no longer
" known to the compofer himfelf; in
" short, I tried to banish all thofe vices
" of the mufical drama, againft which,
" good fenfe and reafon have in vain fo
" long exclaimed.

" I imagined, that the overture ought
" to prepare the audience for the action
" of the piece, and ferve as a kind of
" argument to it; that the inftrumental
" accompaniment should be regulated by
" the intereft of the drama, and not
" leave a void in the dialogue between
" the air and recitative; that they should
" neither break into the fenfe and con-
" nexion of a period, nor wantonly in-
" terrupt the energy or heat of the
" action.

" And laftly, it was my opinion, that
" my firft and chief care, as a dramatic
" compofer, was to aim at a noble fim-
" plicity; and I have accordingly shun-
" ed all parade of unnatural difficulty,
" in favour of clearnefs; nor have I

2   " fought

" fought or ftudied novelty, if it did not
" arife naturally from the fituation of
" the character, and poetical expreffion;
" and there is no rule of compofition,
" which I have not thought it my duty
" to facrifice, in order to favour paffion,
" and produce effects."

From this extract, the reader will in-
fer, that the fymphonies to the fongs
in his opera of *Alcefte*, are few and fhort;
that there are no divifions in the voice-
parts; no formal clofes at the end;
fcarce any but accompanied recitatives,
and that not one *da capo* is to be found
throughout the piece ; which, fay thofe
who have feen it reprefented, was fo
truly theatrical and interefting, that
they could not keep their eyes a moment off the ftage, during the whole
performance, having their attention fo
irritated, and their confternation fo raifed,
that they were kept in perpetual anxiety,
between hope and fear for the event, till
the laft fcene of the drama ; fo that the
mufic only gave energy or foftnefs to the
decla-

declamation, as the different fituations of the feveral characters required. The fyllables were indeed lengthened, and the tones of fpeech afcertained, but fpeech it ftill was, even in the airs, which are almoft all of what the Italians call the *Parlante* or fpeaking kind.

But though M. Gluck ftudies fimple nature fo much in his *cantilena*, or voice-part; yet, in his accompaniments, he is not only often learned, but elaborate; and in this particular, he is even more than a *poet* and *mufician*, he is an excellent *painter*; his inftruments frequently di-lineated the fituation of the actor, and give a high colouring to paffion.

While the chevalier Gluck was fing-ing, count Brühl, a great *dilettante*, join-ed the company; he is a fon of the fa-mous Saxon minifter, and plays in a very mafterly manner upon feveral in-ftruments.

From hence I was carried by lord Stormont to general Valmoden's, the Danifh minifter, quite on the oppofite
fide

fide of the city. There was an affem-
bly of foreign minifters, and his lordfhip did me the honour to prefent me
to the whole *Corps diplomatique.*

Thus ended this bufy and important
day, in which fo much was faid and
done, that it feemed to contain the events
of a much longer period, and I could
hardly perfuade myfelf, at night, upon
recollecting the feveral incidents, that
they had all happened in the fpace of
about twelve hours.

Thurfday 3d. At eleven o' clock this
morning, by appointment, I waited upon
lord Stormont, who was fo kind as to go
with me to the public library; and there,
after being prefented by his lordfhip to
the librarians, and known to have the
honour of being countenanced by him,
I was not only at liberty to enter the
library every day at the ufual hours, but
had admiffion even on holidays, and in
vacation time, when it was denied to
others; and was likewife favoured with
the

the attendance and affiftance of the keepers of the books, at all times, with unlimited politenefs and courtefy.

This library, which has not long been open to the public, is in poffeffion of a very confiderable number of manufcripts, as well as of ancient and modern printed books. The building has been lately enlarged, and the number of books greatly augmented by a purchafe of the library of the late prince Eugene. The celebrated phyfician, baron Van Swieten, lately deceafed, had been many years pricipal librarian, an office which was vacant during my refidence at Vienna.

The principal room of the library is of an immenfe fize, extremely lofty and much ornamented. There are marble ftatues in it of the emperors Charles the Vth, and Leopold. The books have lately undergone a new arrangement, and a new catalogue has been likewife made of them, by one of the *cuftodi*, or keepers. There is a large room fet apart

for

for readers and tranfcribers, and another
for the librarians and their affiftants.

In my way to lord Stormont's, I ftep-
ped into St. Michael's church, in order
to examine the organ, as it is one that
was recommended to my attention, by
Mr. Snetzler, on account of the fingular
difpofition of its keys. This inftrument
has no front, the great pipes are placed,
in an elegant manner, on each fide of the
gallery, and there is a box only in the
middle, of about four feet fquare, for the
keys and ftops; fo that the weft window
is left quite open. The compafs of the
organ, in the manuals, extends only from
double E in the bafe, to C in alt; but
the pedals of moft German organs have
an octave lower than the loweft note of
the keys that are played by the hands,
which is the cafe with this inftrument.
It has forty ftops, and three fets of
keys, which, by a fpring of communi-
cation, can be played all together. The
                                         pipes

pipes are well-toned; and Mr. Wegerer, the prefent organift, though neither remarkable for tafte or fancy, plays in a full and mafterly manner.

St. Croix was another church which I entered this morning, and here I heard a band play during a *meſſa baſſa*; but the mufic was bad, and performance worfe; however, I was hemmed in by the crowd, and forced to ftay and hear it, for near an hour, before I could get out decently.

This morning, the *Abate Taruffi* was fo obliging as to return my vifit. He had already run over my book, and was fufficiently apprized of my purfuits; after a long converfation at my lodging, he carried me to Signor Adolfo Haffe, who lives in a handfome houfe in the fuburbs, called the *Landftraſs*. Signora Fauftina was at the window, and feeing us ftop at the door, came to meet us; I was prefented to her by my conductor. She is a fhort, brown, fenfible, and lively old woman; faid fhe

T   was

was much pleafed to fee a *Cavaliere In-glefe*, as fhe had formerly been honoured with great marks of favour in England.

Signor Haffe foon entered the room; he is tall, and rather large in fize, but it is eafy to imagine, that in his younger days, he muft have been a robuft and fine figure; great gentlenefs and goodnefs appear in his countenance and manners. He feems to have been more ill-treated by time than Fauftina, though he is younger than her by ten years. I pre-fented him a letter, which Sir James Gray had done me the honour to write to him, and which he kept a good while in his hand unread, through politenefs; but during this time the *Abate Taruffi* was giving an account of the views, with which I had already travelled through France and Italy, and which had now brought me to the capital of the German empire.

I had but a fhort time to ftay, being engaged at M. L'Augier's concert, at which,

a 2

as it was made on my account, I should
have been extremely ashamed to arrive
late; and yet, I was so impatient to see
two persons of such distinguished merit,
as Hasse and Faustina, that I could not
resist my desire of going with Signor Taruffi, only for a quarter of an hour. At
length Signor Hasse begged leave to retire to the light, in order to peruse the
letter which I had delivered to him;
during which time his two daughters
came in; they are about twenty-eight
or thirty years of age, not handsome,
but so perfectly well-bred and agreeable
in their manners, that it is easy to discover
immediately, great care has been taken
of their education; they read English,
and speak it a little.

When Miss Davis, who played the Ar-
monica, and her sister, who sung the first
woman's part last year, in the great opera
at Naples, resided at Vienna, they lodged
in the same house with the Hasse family,
and it was during this period, that the

T 2   daughters

daughters of Signor Haffe learned Englifh of the two Mifs Davis's ; and that
this great mafter, by his inftructions, enabled the youngeft of them to fing the
principal part in the firft opera of Europe.

Signor Haffe foon returned, and was
fo eafy and foft in his behaviour, that I
felt myfelf as well acquainted with him
in this quarter of an hour, as if I had
known him twenty years. I faid all
the civil things to him and the Fauftina, that fo fhort a time would allow;
indeed, nothing more than I felt; for
from his works I had received a great
part of my moft early mufical pleafure,
and the delight they afforded me in
youth, has not been diminifhed fince,
by a more general acquaintance with the
writings of other great compofers ; and
therefore faying, that to fee and converfe with him were among the moft interefting concerns which had brought me
to Vienna, that his name was well known

in

in England, and that he had long been
my *magnus Apollo*, was moſt true. He
received all this very humbly, and ſaid,
that he had often been invited, and had
often wiſhed to go to England, as he
had known many perſons of that kingdom, from whom he had received great
civilities.

I aſked him, if it would be poſſible to
obtain a liſt of his works; but he ſaid he
did not know it himſelf. However, he
promiſed to try to recollect the principal
of them, and the Fauſtina offered to
help him. It was with infinite reluctance
that I put an end to my viſit, juſt as we
had made an acquaintance, and the
worſt and formal part of the buſineſs was
over; however, he invited me to come
again as often as I could, enquired my
lodgings, hoped I ſhould reſide ſome
time at Vienna, and other ſuch common
civilities as are little attended to, when
beſtowed by perſons that are indifferent
to us; but which, when uttered by thoſe

T 3　　　　we

we love and reverence, make a deep impreſſion.

From hence I went to Mr. L'Augier's concert, which was begun by the child of eight or nine years old, whom he had mentioned to me before, and who played two difficult leſſons of Scarlatti, with three or four by M. Becke, upon a ſmall, and not good Piano forte. The neatneſs of this child's execution did not ſo much ſurpriſe me, though uncommon, as her expreſſion. All the *pianos* and *fortes* were ſo judiciouſly attended to ; and there was ſuch ſhading off ſome paſſages, and force given to others, as nothing but the beſt teaching, or greateſt natural feeling and ſenſibility could produce. I enquired of Signor Giorgio, an Italian, who attended her, upon what inſtrument ſhe uſually practiſed at home, and was anſwered, " on the Clavichord." This accounts for her expreſſion, and convinces me, that children ſhould learn upon that, or a Piano Forte, very early, and be obliged

7

to give an expreſſion to lady Coventry's
Minuet, or whatever is their firſt tune;
otherwiſe, after long practice on a monotonous harpſichord, however uſeful
for ſtrengthening the hand, the caſe is
hopeleſs.

The company was very numerous, and
compoſed of perſons of great rank; there
was the princeſs Piccolomini, to whom
I had been honoured with a letter; the
duke of Braganza, prince Poniatowſky,
lord Stormont, general Valmoden and
his lady, count Brühl, the duke of Breſciano, &c. &c. It was one of the fineſt aſ-
ſemblies I ever ſaw. When the child
had done playing, M. Mut, a good performer, played a piece on the ſingle harp,
without pedals, which renders it a very
difficult inſtrument, as the performer is
obliged to make the ſemitones by braſs
rings with the left hand, which being
placed at the top of the harp, are not
only hard to get at, but diſagreeable to
hear, from the noiſe, which, by a ſudden

motion of the hand they occasion. The
secret of producing the semitones by pedals, is not yet arrived at Vienna; and
the double harp is utterly unknown there.
This player, though highly esteemed, did
not fulfil all my ideas of the power of
that instrument.

The room was too much crowded for
full pieces : some trios only were played
by Signor Giorgi, a scholar of Tartini,
Conforte, a scholar of Pugnani, and by
count Brühl, who is an excellent performer on many instruments, particularly
the violin, violoncello, and mandoline.
The pieces they executed were composed by Huber, a poor man, who plays
the tenor at the playhouse; but it was
excellent music, simple, clear, good harmony, and frequently fancy and contrivance.

Friday 4. This morning Signor Taruffi did me the honour of presenting me
to the bishop of Ephesus, Monsignore Vis-
conti, the pope's nuncio at the imperial
court,

court, and defcended from the famous
family of Vifconti, which once poffeffed
the fovereignty of Milan * . His excellency is a notable mufician, and fings in
a very pleafing manner; he condefcended
to honour me with a long converfation,
on the fubject of mufic, and of my voyage
into Italy, and even to fhew and fing
with me, fome manufcript canons, of
which he was pleafed to permit me to
take copies; he likewife gave me an Italian fonnet, tranfcribed with his own hand,
which Metaftafio had'written at the defire of the prefent king of Poland, to a
favourite Polifh minuet, fent by that
prince from Warfaw to Vienna for that
purpofe; and he finifhed by inviting me
to dine with him on Sunday.

The Emperor went this day, for a month,
to Laxemberg, where his mother, the

---

* Matthew Vifconti, furnamed the Great, was
acknowledged fovereign of Milan, in 1313; and
John Galeas Vifconti his grandfon, who died in
1402, was the moft celebrated of all the dukes of
Milan.

Empreſs Queen then was ; on this occaſion, almoſt all the firſt people of Vienna were preparing to follow him.
The night before his departure, at a kind
of riding-houſe in the ſuburbs, there was
a ſpecies of tilts and tournaments, which
the Germans call 𝔈𝔞𝔯𝔯𝔬𝔲𝔰𝔢𝔩, 𝔢𝔦𝔫 𝔗𝔥𝔲𝔯𝔫𝔦𝔢𝔯
𝔷𝔲 𝔓𝔣𝔢𝔯𝔡, 𝔬𝔡𝔢𝔯 𝔑𝔦𝔫𝔤𝔢𝔩𝔯𝔢𝔫𝔫𝔢𝔫. The Emperor himſelf was one of the combatants
on this occaſion; after which his imperial
majeſty gave fire-works on the Danube,
at which he was likewiſe preſent; but by
viſiting Signor Haſſe, and by being at M.
L'Augier's concert, I was prevented from
going thither myſelf.

The muſical party, which dined to-day
at lord Stormont's, was ſelect, and in the
higheſt degree entertaining and pleaſing.
It conſiſted of the prince of Poniatowſki,
the duke of Braganza, the Portugueſe
miniſter, count and counteſs Thun, M.
L'Augier, the chevalier, madame and
mademoiſelle Gluck, the Abate Coſta,
&c. This Abate is the extraordinary
muſician

mufician that I mentioned before, who,
difdaining to follow the fteps of others,
has ftruck out a new road, both as compofer and performer, which it is wholly
impoffible to defcribe: all I can fay of his
productions is, that in them melody is
lefs attended to than harmony and uncommon modulation; and that the time
is always difficult to make out, from the
great number of ligatures and fractions;
however, his mufic, when well executed,
which happens but feldom, has a very
fingular and pleafing effect: but it is
certainly too much the work of art to
afford great delight to any ears but thofe
of the learned.

This Abate is poffeffed of as great a
love for independence as M. Rouffeau;
he refufes every kind of affiftance from
the rich, though poor, with fuch inflexi-
bility, that the duke of Braganza and he
had a contention, which lafted a fortnight or three weeks, upon the following.
occa-

occasion, in which, however, the Abate remained victorious.

He wanted very much to correct the imperfections of the finger-board of his guittar, which being strung with catgut, and having three strings to each tone, he found it frequently happen, that these strings, though perfectly in unison, when open, were out of tune when stopped, and this at some of the frets more than others; in order to obviate this, an ingenious mechanic was found, who, with great study and pains, invented moveable frets for each string; but as these were made of brass, and had taken up much of the workman's time to accommodate them, they amounted to four or five florins, a sum the Abate could not afford to pay, and yet he would by no means allow the duke of Braganza to do it. At length the dispute was ended by the duke taking the instrument at prime cost, and the Abate inventing a more cheap
and

and fimple method of correcting the finger-board of another, and this he ef-fected in the following manner : he placed longitudinally, under the upper covering, or veneer, as many rows of catgut ftrings as there were ftrings upon his inftrument; then cutting through the ebony at each fret, and laying thefe under ftrings open, he placed under them little moveable bits of ebony, which rendered the chords upon his inftrument equally perfect in all keys. He can, at pleafure, take off this finger-board laterally; and as his modulation is very learned and extraneous, this expedient was the more neceffary. But his compofitions are not more original in this particular than in the meafure; which, from its fingula-rity, is very difficult to feel, and, confe-quently, to keep with any degree of exactnefs.

He played two movements on his guittar, before dinner, the fubjects of
which,

which, as nearly as I can remember,
were thefe:

Andante.

Prefto.

I fate between this Abate and the
chevalier Gluck, during dinner, and we
all three talked more than we eat. Gluck
recounted to me the difficulties he had
met with in difciplining the band, both
of vocal and inftrumental performers, at
the rehearfals of *Orfeo*, which was the
firft of his operas that was truly dramatic; and even after it had fucceeded with
the public, at the coronation of the prefent

fent Emperor, as king of the Romans, upon which occafion it was firft performed, the Emprefs Queen did not like it; however, hearing every one fpeak favourably of it at court, and finding it the general topic of converfation, fhe determined to give it a fecond hearing, after which her imperial majefty expreffed her approbation of this opera, by fending the poet Calfabigi a diamond ring, and Gluck a rich purfe, lined with a hundred ducats.

A few years fince, a comic opera of Gluck's was performed at the Elector Palatine's theatre, at Schwetzingen : his Electoral highnefs was much ftruck with the mufic, and enquired who had compofed it ; and, upon being informed that it was the production of an honeft German, who loved old hock; " I think, " fays the Elector, he deferves to be " made drink for his trouble ;" and ordered him a tun, not indeed quite fo big

as

as that at Heidelberg, but a very large
one, and full of excellent wine.

After dinner, a duet, for two violins,
by the Abate, was tried by himself and
M. Startzel, an excellent player, and as
good a musician. This performer is remarkably happy in the composition of
ballet and pantomime music, for the
theatre; but the Abate Costa's duo was
so difficult, both in time and style, that
it was never well performed after twenty
or thirty trials.

At length the company, which was
now much encreased, became impatient
to hear mademoiselle Gluck sing, which
she did, sometimes with her uncle's accompaniment, on the harpsichord only,
and sometimes with more instruments,
in so exquisite a manner, that I could not
conceive it possible for any vocal performance to be more perfect.

She executed, admirably, several entire
scenes in her uncle's operas, of which
the

the mufic was fo truly dramatic, pictu-
refque, and well expreffed, that, if my
conjecture be admiffible, of the firft vocal
mufic being the voice of paffion and cry
of nature, the chevalier Gluck's compofitions, and his niece's performance, entirely fulfill that idea.

In fome fcenes of great diftrefs, in
which the human heart is torn by complicated mifery, by " horrors accumu-
late," it is then that M. Gluck, tranfport-
ed beyond the bounds of ordinary genius, gives fuch energy and colouring to
paffion, as to become at once poet,
painter, and mufician. He feems to be
the Michael Angelo of mufic, and is as
happy in painting difficult attitudes, and
fituations of the mind, as that painter
was of the body; indeed, his expreffion
of paffion may fometimes be too ftrong
for common hearers: but,

Il échappe fouvent des fons à la douleur,
Qui font faux pour l'oreille, & font vrais pour le cœur.

DORAT.

U

Be-

Between the vocal parts of this delightful concert, we had some exquisite quartets, by Haydn, executed in the utmost perfection; the first violin by M. Startzler, who played the *Adagios* with uncommon feeling and expression; the second violin by M. Ordonetz; count Brühl played the tenor, and M. Weigel, an excellent performer on the violoncello, the bafe. All who had any fhare in this concert, finding the company attentive, and in a difpofition to be pleafed, were animated to that true pitch of enthufiafm, which, from the ardor of the fire within them, is communicated to others, and fets all around in a blaze; fo that the contention between the performers and hearers, was only who fhould pleafe, and who fhould applaud the moft!

When this mufical repaft was over, I went home with M. L'Augier, to hear a Florentine poet, the Abate Cafti, repeat his own verfes, which he did from memory, for feveral hours, without the

leaft

leaſt ſtop or heſitation. Lord Stormont and moſt of the company came after us, and ſtayed till twelve o'clock. This poet has energy, humour, fire, and invention; he has verſified ſome of Boccaccio's and Voltaire's looſeſt tales, and written other very free ones himſelf.

Saturday 5th. This morning was ſpent in the imperial library, and at the counteſs Thun's, who was on the point of going to Laxemberg for a longer time than I was likely to ſtay at Vienna. This was an afflicting circumſtance, as her houſe was always open to me, and ſhe did every thing in her power to procure me entertainment and ſervices.

She was now ſurrounded by her friends, who, though they were not in my ſituation, but were ſure of ſeeing her again very ſoon, either here, or at Laxemberg; yet they had almoſt tears in their eyes, at the thoughts of loſing her, only for a few days. During this viſit ſhe was ſo kind as to produce all

U 2　　　　　her

her mufical curiofities, for me to hear and
fee, before we parted. Her tafte is admirable, and her execution light, neat,
and feminine; however, fhe told me that
fhe *had* played much better than at prefent, and humouroufly added, that fhe
had had fix children, and that " every
" one of them had taken fomething from
" her," She is a chearful, lively, and
beneficent being, whom every one here
feems to love as a favourite fifter. She
is niece to the once handfome prince
Lobkowitz, who was in England in
1745 and 46, and much connected with
the famous count St. Germain, who
made fo much noife at that time, not
only with his fiddle, but his myfterious
conduct and equivocal character. This
prince is now retired from the world,
and will not fee even his relations and
beft friends for many months together.
He had cultivated mufic fo far, as not
only to play and to judge well, but even
to compofe in a fuperior manner; and
his

his niece gave me feveral of his pieces, which had great merit and novelty, particularly a fong for two orcheftras, which no mafter in Europe need be afhamed of.

In confequence of the application which lord Stormont had kindly made for my being introduced to Metaftafio, his lordfhip had received a very polite meffage from him, with an affurance that he would be glad to fee him and me, any evening his excellency would be pleafed to appoint. This was a moft defirable circumftance, as Metaftafio is ufually inacceffible of an afternoon, to all but his three or four felect friends, and in a morning nothing but a general converfation could be obtained. Lord Stormont being engaged every day till Saturday, fixed on that afternoon for gratifying my defire of feeing and converfing with the favourite poet of every mufician, who has the leaft knowledge of the Italian language. Sa-

turday

turday was now come, and I was big
with expectation for the event.

At fix o'clock in the evening lord
Stormont carried me to him. We found
only one of his particular friends with
him, who is likewife one of the imperial
librarians, and the perfon to whom I
had been introduced at the library, and
who had arranged the vifit.

This great poet is lodged, as many
other great poets have been before him,
in a very exalted fituation, up no lefs
than four pair of ftairs. Whether modern bards prefer the fublimity of this
abode, on account of its being fomewhat
on a level with Mount Parnaffus, nearer
their fire Apollo, or in the neighbourhood of gods in general, I fhall not determine; but a more plain and humble
reafon can be affigned for Metaftafio's
habitation being " twice two ftories
high," if we confider the peculiar prerogative which the emperor enjoys at
Vienna,

Vienna, of appropriating, to the ufe of the officers of his court and army, the *firſt floor* of every houfe and palace in that city, fix or eight privileged places only excepted. On this account, princes, ambaffadors, and nobles, ufually inhabit the fecond ftories; and the third, fourth, and even fifth floors, the houfes being very large and high, are well fitted up, for the reception of opulent and noble families; and our poet, though he occupies that part of a houfe, which, in England, is thought only fit for domeftics to fleep in, has, neverthelefs, an exceeding good and elegant apartment, in which an imperial laureate may, with all due dignity, hold dalliance with the Mufes.

He received us with the utmoft chearfulnefs and good-breeding; and I was no lefs aftonifhed than pleafed at finding him look fo well: he does not feem more than fifty years of age, though he is at

leaſt

leaſt ſeventy-two *; and, for that time of
life, he is the handſomeſt man I ever beheld
There are painted on his countenance
all the genius, goodneſs, propriety, benevolence, and rectitude, which conſtantly
characteriſe his writings.   I could not
keep my eyes off his face, it was ſo
pleaſing and worthy of contemplation.
His converſation was of a piece with his
appearance : polite, eaſy, and lively.
We got him to open upon muſic much
more than we expected ; for, in general,
he avoids entering deep into any particular ſubject.   He ſet off, however, by
ſaying, that he could furniſh me with
very few new lights upon my ſubject,
as he had never conſidered it with ſufficient attention ; however, in the courſe
of our converſation, he diſcovered him-

* There is an edition of his opera of Giuſtino
extant, which was printed in 1713 ; and as he was
ſaid to have been fourteen when he wrote that poem,
it throws his birth into the laſt century.

ſelf

felf to have a very good general knowledge both of the hiftory and theory of
mufic; and I was very much flattered
to find his fentiments correfpond with
my own in many doubtful particulars.

We difcuffed the following fubjects:
the mufical fcales of the ancient Greeks;
their melody, chorus, modes, and declamation; the origin of modern harmony and operas; the fondnefs for fugues
in the laft century, and for noife in
this, &c. &c.

He feems rather pleafed with Mr.
Hoole's tranflation of the two firft volumes of his works; but thinks, with
me, that if he has failed, it is more in
the fongs than recitatives: however, in
excufe for Mr. Hoole, he fays, that the
cafe is hopelefs in tranflating Italian
poetry, for the language itfelf is fo foft
and mufical, that no other can furnifh
words equivalent in fweetnefs. He likes
no one of the many thoufand tranflations
and imitations of his *Grazi e agl'Inganni
tuoi.*

tuoi. I afked him, if he was author of
a duo to thefe words, which I had procured many years ago, and fung him the
two or three firft bars; and he faid,
" fomething like it."

We talked of the different editions of
his works; he thinks thofe of Paris and
Turin, in ten volumes, are the moft
complete and correct. Thefe contain all
that he intended to publifh, except the
opera of *Ruggiero*, performed at Milan
laft year; lord Stormont lamented that
the pieces were not arranged in an exact
chronological order; but Metaftafio faid,
that it was of little moment to the public whether he wrote *Artaferfe*, or *Didone*
firft; however, he confeffed, that there
were fome particulars which gave birth
to feveral of thefe pieces, which perhaps
fhould be known.

Here he told us, that when his miftrefs, the Emprefs Queen was going to be
married to the duke of Lorrain, he was
applied to for an opera on the occafion,
and

2

and he had only eighteen days allowed
him to write it in. He immediately
cried out, that it was impoſſible; but,
when he got home, he ſketched out the
ſtory of *Achilles in Sciros*; he delineated
a kind of argument upon a large ſheet of
paper; here he was to begin; thus far
the firſt act; theſe the incidents of the ſecond, and this, the cataſtrophe of the
third. Then he diſtributed buſineſs to
his ſeveral characters; here a ſong, here
a duo, and here a ſoliloquy. He then
proceeded to write the dialogue, and to
divide it into ſcenes, which were ſeverally given to the compoſer the moment
they were finiſhed, and by him to the
performer to be got by heart. For the
eighteen days included the whole arrangement of poetry, muſic, dancing, ſcenes,
and decorations.

He ſaid, that neceſſity frequently augmented our powers, and forced us to perform, not only what we thought ourſelves
incapable of, but in a much more expedi-
tious,

tious, and often in a better manner, than the operations of our choice and leisure ; he added, that *Hypermnestra* was produced in nine days, and it is remarkable, that *Achilles* and *Hypermnestra* are two of Metastasio's best dramas.

Lord Stormont asked if he had ever set any of his operas to music himself, and he answered, that he was not musician sufficient; he had, indeed, now and then given a composer the *motivo*, or subject of an air, to shew how he wished it should express his words ; but no more. His lordship told him, that old Fontenelle had said, in his hearing, that no musical drama would be perfect, or interesting, till the poet and musician were one, as in ancient times; and that when Rousseau's *Devin du Village* came out, and so delighted every hearer, the literary patriarch Fontenelle, attributed its success to that union of poet and musician.

But Metastasio said, that musical composition, was now an affair of so much

skill

skill and science, in regard to counterpoint, the knowledge of inftruments, the powers of a finger, and other particulars, that it required too much time and application for a modern poet, or man of letters, to acquire them.

He faid, he did not think there that was now one finger left, who could fuftain the voice in the manner the old fingers were ufed to do. I endeavoured to ac- count for this, and he agreed with me, that theatrical mufic was become too inftrumental; and that the cantatas of the beginning of this century, which were fung with no other accompani- ment than a harpfichord or violoncello, required better finging than the prefent fongs, in which the noify accompani- ments can hide defects as well as beau- ties, and give relief to a finger.

He feemed to think, that the mufic of the laft age was in general too full of *fugues*, of parts, and contrivances, to be felt or underftood, except by artifts. All

I   the

the different movements of the several
parts, their inverfions and divifions, he
faid, were unnatural, and, by covering
and deforming the melody, only occafion=
ed confufion.

He confirmed to me the ftory of his
having been forced, by Gravina, to tranflate the whole Iliad of Homer into Italian *Ottave Rime*, at twelve years old.
He likewife mentioned his having made
verfes *all' improvvifa* when young; but
that he had difcontinued the practice
before he was feventeen.

Several jokes efcaped him in the courfe
of our converfation, and he was equally
chearful, polite, and attentive, the whole
time. We ftayed with him juft two
hours; and, at my going away, he fhook
me by the hand, enquired where I lodged, and faid he would wait on me; but
I begged he would not give himfelf that
trouble, faying that I fhould be perfectly
happy in a permiffion to pay my refpects
to him again: he then defired me to
come

come whenever I pleafed, and affured me that he fhould be always glad to fee me.

He called for candles, and faid it was fo dark that our words could not find the way to their deftination. He fpoke to his fervant in German, ein Licht: upon which I afked him if he had had patience to learn that language? he replied, " A " few words only, to fave my life:" meaning to afk for neceffaries, or he fhould have been ftarved to death.

Lord Stormont faid that news of a re-volution in Sweden had arrived that morning. This occafioned a political converfation for fome time, which I wifhed very much to have changed——— *Ecco*, fays Metaftafio, turning to me, *un' altra fcena per la drama!* Here's a new fcene for the drama! He obferved, that the interefts of mankind were fo various and fo oppofite, and even a man's own conceptions were fo frequently at ftrife

with

with themfelves, that it was not poffible for the world to go on without thefe fudden events, which fhould furprife no one who confiders how full the head of man is of contradictions and caprice.

Sunday morning, 6th. In my way to the nuncio's, whence I was to fet off with the Abate Taruffi, to make Metaftafio another vifit, I was ftopt by a proceffion of, literally, two or three miles long, finging a hymn to the Virgin, in three parts, and repeating each ftanza after the priefts, in the van, at equal diftances; fo that the inftant one company had done, it was taken up by another behind, till it came to the women in the rear, who, likewife, at equal diftances, repeated, in three parts, the few fimple notes of this hymn; and even after them it was repeated by girls, who were the laft perfons in the proceffion. When thefe had done, it was begun again by the priefts. The melody was fomething like this:

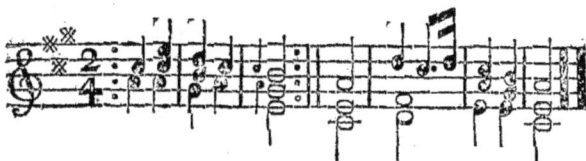

I was told by an Italian at Vienna, that the Auftrians are extremely addicted to proceffions, *portatiffimi alle proceffioni.* There were five or fix of thefe proceffions this morning; and yet it is obferved, that they are much lefs frequent than formerly : however, not a day paffed, while I remained in this city, without one or more to fome church or convent: but all this helps to teach the people to fing in different parts.

When Signor Taruffi and I arrived at Metaftafio's levee, we found about fix or eight perfons with him, chiefly Italians ; his excellency the governor of the city, came in after us. The great poet received me very courteoufly, and placed me on a fopha, juft by him. I now delivered him a letter from Mingotti, and Signor Taruffi read Mr. Baret-

X

ti's

ti's letter concerning me; so that here were many claims upon him: however lord Stormont had done the business completely, without any other help.

After the perusal of these letters, the conversation turned upon the poet Migliavacca, of Milan, who has long been laureate to the court of Dresden. Metastasio mentioned him with great praise: he said that he was a man of infinite knowledge, and of great genius; yet he wrote but little, for he had ideas of perfection which neither himself, nor perhaps any one else, could satisfy; besides, added Metastasio, " he has had but little " practice. And all is *habit* in mankind, " even *virtue itself*."

The discourse then became general and miscellaneous, till the arrival of a young lady, who was received by the whole company with great respect. She was well dressed, and had a very elegant appearance: this was Signora Martinetz, sister to Signor Martinetz, deputy
librarian

librarian at the imperial library, whofe
father was an old friend of Metaftafio.
She was born in the houfe in which he
now lives, and educated under his eye:
her parents were Neapolitans, but the
name is Spanifh, as the family originally
was.

After the high encomiums beftowed
by the Abate Taruffi on the talents of
this young lady, I was very defirous of
hearing and converfing with her; and
Metaftafio was foon fo obliging as to pro-
pofe her fitting down to the harpfichord,
which fhe immediately did, in a graceful
manner, without the parade of diffidence,
or the trouble of importunity. Her performance indeed furpaffed all that I had
been made to expect. She fung two
airs of her own compofition, to words of
Metaftafio, which fhe accompanied on
the harpfichord, in a very judicious and
mafterly manner; and, in playing the
ritornels, I could difcover a very brilliant
finger.

The airs were very well written, in a
modern ftyle; but neither common, nor
unnaturally new. The words were well
fet, the melody was fimple, and great
room was left for expreffion and embellifhment; but her voice and manner of
finging, both delighted and aftonifhed
me! I can readily fubfcribe to what Metaftafio fays, that it is a ftyle of finging
which no longer fubfifts elfewhere, as
it requires too much pains and patience
for modern profeffors: *è perduta la fcuola;
non fi trova quefta maniera di cantar; do-
manda troppa pena per i profeffori d'oggi
dì.* I fhould fuppofe that Piftocco, Bernacchi, and the old fchool of finging, in
the time of cantatas, fuftained, divided
the voice by minute intervals, and expreffed
words in this manner, which is not to
be defcribed: common language cannot
exprefs uncommon effects. To fay that
her voice was naturally well-toned and
fweet, that fhe had an excellent fhake,
a perfect intonation, a facility of executing

cuting the moſt rapid and difficult paſ-
fages, and a touching expreſſion, would
be to fay no more than I have already
faid, and with truth, of others; but here
I want words that would ſtill encreaſe
the fignificance and energy of theſe ex-
preſſions. The Italian augmentatives
would, perhaps, gratify my wiſh, if I
were writing in that language; but as
that is not the caſe, let me only add, that
in the *portamento*, and diviſions of tones
and femi-tones into infinitely minute
parts, and yet always ſtopping upon the
exact fundamental, Signora Martinetz was
more perfect than any finger I had ever
heard : her cadences too, of this kind,
were very learned, and truly pathetic
and pleafing.

After theſe two fongs, ſhe played a
very difficult leſſon, of her own compofition, on the harpfichord, with great
rapidity and precifion. She has compoſed a *Miferere*, in four parts, with fe-

X 3　　　　　　veral

veral Pfalms, in eight parts, and is a moſt excellent contrapuntiſt.

The company broke up ſooner than I wiſhed, as it was Metaſtaſio's time for going to maſs. During this viſit, I diſcovered that Signora Martinetz, among her other accompliſhments, both reads and ſpeaks Engliſh. She invited me to come again, as did the divine poet; ſo that I now regarded myſelf as *amico della caſa.*

The imperial laureate was carried to church in a very elegant carriage, which I rejoiced to ſee : his talents and his virtues merit all that can be done for him. His penſion is about five hundred pounds ſterling a year, which, with his regular life and œconomy, enables him to live in a very reputable, though not ſplendid manner.

After dining with his excellency Monſignore Viſconti, his ſecretary carried me a ſecond time to the houſe of Signor Haſſe,

Haſſe, in the Landſtraß, the prettieſt of all the Fauxbourgs of Vienna. It is a delightful drive of about a mile and half beyond the gates, and is within the lines, though without the walls; chiefly through one ſtreet, with frequent openings, that let palaces, churches, and fine houſes, into the proſpect.

We found all the family at home, and were very chearful and ſocial. Signora Fauſtina is very converſable, and is ſtill poſſeſſed of much curioſity concerning what is tranſacting in the world. She has likewiſe good remains, for ſeventy-two, of that beauty for which ſhe was ſo much celebrated in her youth, but none of her fine voice! I aſked her to ſing—*Ah non poſſo!—hò perduto tutte le mie facoltà.* Alas! I am no longer able, ſaid ſhe, I have loſt all my faculties.

I was extremely captivated with the converſation of Signor Haſſe. He was eaſy, communicative, and rational; equally free from pedantry, pride, and preju-

X 4   dice.

dice. He spoke ill of no one; but, on the contrary, did justice to the talents of several composers that were occasionally named, even to those of Porpora; who, though his first master, was ever after his greatest rival. He thinks, with Metastasio, that the good school for singing is lost; and says, that since the time of Pistocco, Bernacchi, and Porpora, no great scholars have been made.

I asked him again for a list of his works, and he told me that he had set all the operas of Metastasio, except *Temistocle*; some of them three or four times over, and almost all of them twice: besides these, he had set many operas, written by Apostolo Zeno; for, in his youth, Metastasio did not write fast enough for him. To these compositions for the theatre, must be added fourteen or fifteen *Oratorios*, with *Masses, Misereres, Stabat Maters,* and *Salve Reginas,* for the church. Besides all which, he added, that his *Cantatas, Serenatas, Inter-*

mez-

mezzos, and *Duets* for voices; his trios, quartets, and concertos, for inftruments, were fo numerous, that he fhould not know many of them again, if he was either to fee or hear them. He modeftly compared himfelf to animals of the greateft fecundity, whofe progeny were either deftroyed during infancy, or abandoned to chance; and added, that he, like other bad fathers, had more pleafure in producing, than in preferving his off-fpring. However, this cenfure muft be confined to the offspring of his brain, for, as I before obferved, he has taken great care of the education of his daughters.

During this vifit, thefe young ladies were fo obliging as to fing to me a *Salve Regina*, lately fet by their father, in *duo*. It is an exquifite compofition, full of grace, tafte, and propriety.

One of his daughters has a fweet *foprano voce di camera*, of which the tone is delicate and interefting : the other has

a rich

a rich and powerful *contralto* voice, fit
for any church or theatre in Europe:
both have good ſhakes, and ſuch an expreſſion, taſte, and ſteadineſs, as it is natural to expect in the daughters and ſcholars of Signor Haſſe and Signora Fauſtina.

After the *Salve Regina*, theſe excellent
performers ſung ſeveral airs, in different
ſtyles, of their father's compoſition, in
a truly noble and elegant manner.

Signor Haſſe is ſo much afflicted with
the gout, that his fingers are ſtiff, and
diſtorted with it; and yet there are remains of a great player, in his manner
of touching the harpſichord, and of accompanying; nor is it for want of knowing
learned, extraneous, and equivocal modulation, that he is ſo ſparing of it in
his works.   He played me an extempore
Toccato or *Capriccio,* in which he introduced ſome that was truly wonderful;
but he has too ſound a judgment, to la-
viſh upon common and trivial occaſions,
what

what fhould be referved for extraordinary purpofes. His modulation is, in
general, fimple, his melody natural, his
accompaniments free from confufion ;
and, leaving to fops and pedants all
that frights, aftonifhes, and perplexes,
he lets no other arts be difcoverable in
his compofitions, than thofe of pleafing
the ear, and of fatisfying the under-
ftanding.

His daughters complain of want of
practice, and fay they hardly ever fing ;
for their father is always either ill or
bufy.

He is going, next fpring, to Venice,
the birth-place of Signora Fauftina ; and
it feems as if they both had determined
to fpend the reft of their days there.

It does not appear that Signor Haffe
has at prefent either penfion or employment at Vienna. He had great loffes
during the laft war ; all his books, manufcripts, and effects were burned at the
bombardment of Drefden, by the King
of

of Pruffia, to a very confiderable amount.
He was going to print a complete edition of all his works; the late king of
Poland promifed to be at the expence of
paper and prefs; but after M. Breitkopf,
of Leipzig, had made a beginning, and
got together materials for the whole impreffion, the war broke out, and put
an end to all his hopes from this enterprize, and to thofe of the public. He,
however, does great juftice to the mufical talents of the King of Pruffia; and
is even fo candid, as to fay, that he
believes, if his majefty had known
that contingencies would have obliged
him to bombard Drefden, he would pre-
vioufly have apprized him of it, that
he might have faved his effects.

Fauftina, who is a living volume of
mufical hiftory, furnifhed me with many
anecdotes of her cotemporary performers,
She fpoke much of Handel's great ftyle
of playing the harpfichord and organ
when fhe was in England, and faid, fhe

2   remem-

remembered Farinelli's coming to Venice, in the year 1728, and the rapture and astonishment with which he was then heard.

Monday 7th. This whole morning was spent in the public library, in search of old Missals, musical treatises, and compositions. M. Martinetz, brother to the young lady whom I had heard sing and play her own compositions so well at Metastasio's, attended and assisted me the whole time. I asked him, of whom his sister learned music, and where she had acquired her expressive manner of singing; he said, she had had several masters to teach her the grammar and mechanism of music; but that it was Metastasio who had done the rest.

I obtained the following particulars from a person of high rank, who has resided at Vienna so long, that he is perfectly acquainted with the history of musical people.

The

The great finger fignora Tefi, who was a celebrated performer, upwards of fifty years ago, lives here; fhe is now more than eighty, but has long quitted the ftage. She has been very fprightly in her day, and yet is at prefent in high favour with the Emprefs Queen. Her ftory is fomewhat fingular. She was connected with a certain count, a man of great quality and diftinction, whofe fondnefs, encreafed by enjoyment, to fuch a degree as to determine him to marry her: a much more uncommon refolution in a perfon of high birth on the continent than in England. She tried to diffuade him; enumerated all the bad confequences of fuch an alliance; but he would liften to no reafoning, nor take any denial. Finding all remonftrances vain, fhe left him one morning, went into a neighbouring ftreet, and addreffing herfelf to a poor labouring man, a journeyman baker, faid fhe would give him fifty ducats if he would marry her; not

with

with a view to their cohabiting together, but to ferve a prefent purpofe. The poor man readily confented to become her nominal hufband : accordingly they were formally married ; and when the count renewed his folicitations, fhe told him it was now utterly impoffible to grant his requeft, for fhe was already the wife of another ; a facrifice fhe had made to his fame and family.

Since this time fhe has lived, many years, with a man of great rank at Vienna, of near her own age ; probably in a very chafte and innocent manner.

The Teuberinn, another celebrated opera finger, likewife refides here ; but, fhe is peremptorily ordered by her phyfician never to fing again. Her health was fo impaired in Ruffia, that it is pronounced by the faculty, that the exercife of her former profeffion would certainly be fatal to her.

It was the Tefi who taught both the Teuberinn and De Amici to fing as well

as

as to act. She had in her youth been
very superior to all her cotemporaries in
both capacities of singer and actress, and
was afterwards remarkably happy in con-
veying instructions to her pupils.

Sept. 8. I expected that this would
be a fruitless day, with regard to my
musical researches; it was a great festival; the library was shut up, and all the
world was in *gala*, and at their devotions;
it is pleasant enough to walk the streets
on these days, and see the people, freed
from toil and care, appear all clean and
chearful.

The Portuguese abate called on me
early in the morning, and after a long
musical discourse, he invited me to his
room, to hear some of his compositions
on the guittar, in peace and quiet, which
it had been impossible to do at lord
Stormont's; he hates mortally more than
two or three hearers at a time. I followed him to his garret, more than twice two
stories high; here he played the same

pieces

pieces as at lord Stormont's, but with more effect, in ftill filence. He is quite original in his ideas and modulation, but repeats his paffages too often.

From hence, I went to St. Stephen's cathedral, where high mafs was juft begun, on account of its being the Nativity of the Virgin. The band was reinforced; there were more than the ufual number of inftruments, as well as voices; but the organ was infufferably out of tune, which contaminated the whole performance. In other refpects, the mufic, which was chiefly by Colonna, was excellent in its kind, confifting of fugues well worked, much in Handel's way, with a bold and active bafe. Some fine effects were produced with the *fortes* and *pianos,* by ftriking the firft note of a bar loud, the reft foft,

F. P.   F. P.

and by introducing a piece of pathetic

for

for voices only, in the middle of a noify, full, inftrumental chorus.

There was a girl, who fung a folo verfe, in the *Credo*, extremely well, in a *mezzo foprano* voice; her fhake and ftyle of finging were good. There were like-wife feveral fymphonies for inftruments only, compofed by M. Hofman, *maeftro di capella* of this church, which were well written and well executed, except that the hateful four organ, poifoned all whenever it played. In the mufic com-pofed by M. Hofman, though there was great art and contrivance, yet the mo-dulation was natural, and the melody fmooth and elegant. "As much art as "you pleafe in your mufic, gentlemen", faid I, frequently, to the Germans, "provided it be united with nature; and "even in a marriage between art and "nature, I fhould always wifh the lady "to wear the breeches ."

In the afternoon, I called on M. L'Augier, and there, among other com-

pany

pany met again with the Florentine poet, Abate Cafti, who repeated feveral of his poems, particularly, a tale from Voltaire, called *L'Art d'élever une Fille*; which was extremely arch and comic.

M. L'Augier being in the fervice of the court, was obliged to attend the emperor the next day at Laxemberg; I was forry to lofe him, as his houfe was an excellent retreat, when I could fpare time to enjoy it; and his converfation concerning mufic and muficians was in a particular manner entertaining and profitable.

He blamed me much for not continuing the whole winter at Vienna, but if I had ftayed a full year in every great city of Europe, the inhabitants would have thought its curiofities and importance merited ftill more attention; and what a longevity muft I be poffeffed of, to gratify fuch patriotifm? and when would my enquiries, and my hiftory end? When M. L'Augier faid, that Vienna deferved a much longer vifit, I afked him, after Haffe, Gluck, and Wagenfeil, what

more

more great muficians were to be found
in this city? Haydn, Ditters, and Scarlatti, the nephew to Dominico Scarlatti,
were out of town; I knew there were
Gafman, Vanhall, Hofmann, Mancini;
and he added Kohaut, a great lutanift,
La Motte, a violinift, and Venturini, a
hautboy; but moft of thefe I could fee
and hear, before my departure. To get
admiffion into the archives of the imperial chapel, was now the moft important
bufinefs I had to tranfact; and my Por-
tuguefe Abate had promifed to introduce
me to M. Gafman, the Emperor's *maeftro
di capella*, for that purpofe.

After quitting M. L'Augier, I vifited
M. Wagenfeil, where I found my good
friend the Abate Cofta, who had played
the precurfor, and prepared him for my
arrival.

Wagenfeil is rather in years, thin, and
infirm; he was confined to his couch,
but received me very politely, and converfed freely on the fubject of mufic for
a con-

for a confiderable time; he has a great
refpect for Handel, and fpeaks of fome
of his works with rapture; he could
not ftir from his feat, and his left hand
had been fo ill treated by the gout,
that he was hardly able to move two
of his fingers. However, at my ur-
gent requeft, he had a harpfichord
wheeled to him, and he played me feveral *capriccios*, and pieces of his own
compofition, in a very fpirited and mafterly manner; and though I can eafily
believe, that he once played better; yet,
he had fufficient fire and fancy left to
pleafe and entertain, though not to furprife me very much; he was fo obliging as
to promife me copies of feveral of his
manufcript compofitions for the harpfichord, and to make a fmall mufical
party for me, at his houfe, in order to
give me an opportunity of hearing fome
of his fcholars.

He has been confined to his room thefe
feven years by a lamenefs, which came

Y 3

on

on by degrees in a very uncommon manner. The finews of his right thigh are
contracted, and the circulation ftopt; fo
that it is become incurably withered,
and ufelefs. He is fifty-eight years of
age, was a fcholar of Fux, and many years
mafter to the Emprefs Queen, on which
account he ftill enjoys a penfion of fifteen
hundred florins a-year. He is now nominal mafter to the arch-duchefles, for
which he has, likewife, a fmall penfion.

Thefe are fortunate circumftances for
a perfon totally incapable of quitting his
room, in order to exercife his profeffion.
However, he teaches at home, and compofes, by which he fomewhat augments
his income; and, as he is luckily a fingle
man, and Vienna not a dear place for the
natives to live in, he may be fuppofed in
eafy circumftances.

The diverfions for the common people of this place, are fuch as feem hardly
fit for a civilized and polifhed nation to
allow. Particularly the *combats*, as they

are

are called, or baiting of wild beafts, in a
manner much more favage and ferocious
than our bull-baiting, throwing at cocks,
and prize-fighting of old, to which the
legiflature has fo wifely and humanely
put a ftop*.

Thefe

---

* The moft exact and leaft fufpicious defcription
I can give of thefe diverfions will be literally to
tranflate a hand-bill, fuch as is diftributed through
the ftreets every Sunday and feftival.

" This day, by imperial licence, in the great
" amphitheatre, at five o'clock will begin the fol-
" lowing diverfions.

" 1ft. A wild Hungarian ox, in full fire,
" (that is, with fire under his tail, and crackers
" faftened to his ears and horns, and to other
" parts of his body), will be fet upon by dogs.

" 2d. A wild boar will, in the fame manner,
" be baited by dogs.

" 3d. " A great bear will, immediately after,
" be torn by dogs.

" 4th. A wolf will be hunted by dogs of the
" fleeteft kind.

5th. " A very furious and enraged wild bull
" from Hungary, will be attacked by fierce and
" hungry dogs.

6th. " A frefh bear will be attacked by hounds.

Y 4

7th. " Will

Thefe barbarous fpectacles, are ufually attended by two or three thoufand people, among whom are a great number of ladies!

Wednefday 9th. This morning, I went, with the Abate Cofta, to M. Gafman, *maeftro di capella del corte imperiale.* He was very obliging, and did me the favour to fhew me all his curious books and manufcript compofitions.

He furprifed me much by the number of fugues, and choruffes, which he fhewed me of a very learned and fingular conftruction, which he had made as exercifes

and

7th. " Will appear a fierce wild boar, juft " caught, which will now be baited for the firft " time, by dogs defended with iron armour.

8th. " A beautiful African tyger.

9th. " This will be changed for a bear.

10th. " A frefh and fierce Hungarian ox.

11th. " And laftly, a furious and hungry bear, " which has had no food for eight days, will at- " tack a young wild bull, and eat him alive up- " on the fpot; and if he is unable to complete " the bufinefs, a wolf will be ready to help him."

and ftudies. Some of them were compofed in two or three different *times,* as
well as upon two or three different *fubjects;* and feveral of thefe, he faid, the
emperor had practifed.

M. Gafman is accufed by fome of
want of fire in his theatrical compofitions; but the gravity of his ftyle is eafily accounted for, by the time and pains
he muft have beftowed on church mufic.
To aim at equal perfection in both, is
trying to ferve God and Mammon; and
thofe excellent compofers for the church,
whofe works have furvived them, fuch as
Paleftrina, Tallis, Birde, Allegri, Bene-
voli, Colonna, Caldara, Lotti, Perti, and
Fux, have confined themfelves wholly to
the church ftyle. Aleffandro Scarlatti,
Handel, Pergolefi, and Jomelli, are excep-
tions. But, in general, thofe fucceed beft
in writing for the church, ftage, or chamber, who accuftom themfelves to that
particular fpecies of compofition only.

I do not call every modern oratorio,
mafs, or motet, *church mufic;* as the fame
compofitions

compositions to different words would do equally well, indeed often better, for the ftage. But by *Mufica di Chiefa*, properly fo called, I mean grave and fcientific compofitions for voices only, of which the excellence confifts more in good harmony, learned modulation, and fugues upon ingenious and fober fubjects, than in light airs and turbulent accompaniments.

There are two mufical archives or libraries belonging to the Imperial theatre and chapel. Of one, the emperor had taken away the key; but it contained only the works of compofers, who had flourifhed in the prefent century, fuch as Fux, Telemann, Handel, and Porpora. Of the other, M. Gafman had the key, and promifed to go with me thither the next day: the public library occupied the reft of this.

There was mufic every day, during dinner, and in the evening at the inn, where I lodged, which was the Golden Ox;

Ox; but it was ufually bad, particularly that of a band of wind inftruments, which conftantly attended the ordinary. This confifted of French horns, clarinets, hautboys, and baffoons; all fo miferably out of tune, that I wifhed them a hundred miles off.

In general I did not find that delicacy of ear among the German ftreet-muficians, which I had met with in people of the fame rank and profeffion in Italy. The church organs being almoft always out of tune here, may be occafioned by the parfimony or negligence of the clergy, bifhop, or fuperior of a church or convent; but the being, or ftopping, in or out of tune, among ftreet muficians, muft depend on themfelves, and on their organs being *acute* or *obtufe.*

It is perhaps not eafy to determine what kind of air is moft fit for the propagation of mufical found; whether thick or thin, moift or dry; and if this were determined, it might ftill be doubted in

what

what kind of air mufic would be heard
to the greateft advantage, becaufe, poffibly, that air which is moft favourable to
the tranfmiffion of found, abftractedly
confidered, may render the organs, by
which it is perceived, lefs acutely fenfible.

Thurfday 10th. This morning Signor
Mancini, of Bologna, finging mafter to
the Imperial court and family, was fo
obliging, at the requeft of the auditor
Taruffi, as to call on me at my lodgings.
He was a fcholar of Bernacchi, and has
been fifteen years in the fervice of this
court. He has taught eight of the arch-
dutcheffes to fing, moft of whom, he fays,
had good voices, and had made a confiderable progrefs, particularly the princefs of Parma, and the arch-dutchefs
Elizabeth, who have good fhakes, a
good *portamento*, and great facility of executing fwift divifions.

Signor Mancini fpeaks with much intelligence of his art, and I was greatly
                                        pleafed

pleated with his converfation. He has
for fome time been writing a book upon
the art of finging, which is in great for-
wardnefs; and it is hoped that a perfon
of fuch confummate knowledge, and long
experience, will not keep from the world
a work fo much wanted, as a well-writ-
ten, profound, and, at the fame time,
practical treatife on the art of finging.

I obtained from this able profeffor, a
lift of the Piftocco and Bernacchi fchool.
Bernacchi was the fcholar of Piftocco,
but his voice was never naturally good;
and when he fung, for the firft time, at
a church in Bologna, he was fo very much
difliked, that fome of his acquaintance
peremptorily told him, he fhould leave off
finging, unlefs he could perform better.
This ftimulated and piqued him to take
uncommon pains, well knowing that there
was then no poffibility of changing his profeffion : a caftrato has feldom ftrength or
fpirit fufficient for any other employment
than that of mufic; he therefore went ferioufly

rioufly to work, and, by a fevere ftudy,
acquired a ftyle and manner of finging,
which was afterwards the ftandard of
perfection in that art.

His principal fcholars were Antonio
Pafi, Geo. Battifta Minelli, Bartolomeo
di Faenza, Mancini, and Guarducci.

Signor Mancini thinks it practicable,
with time and patience, not only to give
a fhake where nature has denied it, but
even to give voice ; that is, to make a bad
one tolerable, and an indifferent one
good, as well as to extend the compafs :
always obferving the natural tendency of
the organ.

He told me of a curious operation performed frequently at Naples, of cutting
the glands of the throat, when fo in-
flated, or big, as to obftruct the free paffage of the voice.

For the fhake, he thinks it ruined nine-
ty-nine times out of a hundred, by too
much impatience and precipitation, both
in

in the mafter and fcholar; and many
who can execute paffages, which require
the fame motion of the larynx as the
fhake, have notwithftanding never acquired one. There is no accounting for
this, but from the neglect of the mafter
to ftudy nature, and avail himfelf of thefe
paffages, which, by continuity, would
become real fhakes.

On quitting Signor Mancini, I haftened
to M. Gafman, who was waiting to carry
me to the Imperial mufical library. I
found in it an immenfe collection of
mufical authors, but in fuch diforder,
that their contents are, at prefent, almoft
wholly unknown. However, M. Gaf-
man has begun a catalogue, and is promifed, by the Emperor, a large and
more commodious room for thefe books,
than the prefent, in which they are
promifcuoufly piled, one on another, in
the moft confufed manner imaginable.
Yet I found a great number of curious

rious things from the beginning of coun=
terpoint to the prefent time. Indeed the
quantity of mufic here, of the Emperor
Leopold's collecting, which is uniformly
bound, in white vellum, with his arms
on the back, is almoft incredible; it
feems to be all that Italy and Germany
had then produced : and for operas, in
fcore, and parts, the lift of fuch only as
have been performed at this court, would
fill a folio volume.

M. Gafman has affured me, that in the
courfe of his writing a complete catalogue, he will remark all that is curious
in this collection, both as to theory and
practice, and will communicate it to me
by letter ; and for this purpofe he defired
me to give him my addrefs in England,
which I wrote on parchment, and left in
the library.

I went again this afternoon to Wagenfeil's ; he had with him a little girl,
his fcholar, about eleven or twelve years
old,

old, with whom he played duets upon two harpſichords, which had a very good effect. The child's performance was very neat and ſteady. M. Wagenſeil was ſo kind as to promiſe, at my requeſt, to get, if poſſible, ſome of his duets, and other new pieces, tranſcribed for me by Sunday, when I was to return to him again, to hear them accompanied by violins, and to take my leave: there was a young count here, another of his ſcholars, who had a very rapid finger, and who exe‑cuted ſome very difficult harpſichord leſſons with great preciſion. My friend, the ingenious and worthy Portugueſe abate, was likewiſe of the party.

From hence I went to the opera, which was *i Rovinati*, compoſed by Gaſman, who was at the harpſichord. Whether his civilities in the morning had operated ſecretly on my mind and ears, I cannot tell: but this muſic pleaſed me much more than any of his compoſitions which I had heard before. There was a con‑

Z   traſt,

traſt, an oppoſition and diſſimilitude of movements and paſſages, by which one contributed to the advantage and effect of another, that was charming ; and the inſtrumental parts were judiciouſly and ingeniouſly worked.

A ſong of Clementina Baglioni, and a ſcolding *duo* between her and the ſecond woman, who was a German, and who, indeed, performed but indifferently, were encored. The men who ſung to-night pleaſed me more than thoſe I had heard before; a tenor, in particular, diſ-covered much taſte, and had a pleaſing, though not powerful voice. Theſe vague accounts of anonymous ſingers, will afford the reader but ſmall ſatisfaction ; but it is all I am able to give him of performers of a lower order, as the names of ſingers are never printed in the *dramatis perſonæ* of Italian operas in Germany, and me-mory ſeldom aſſiſts us in retaining the names of either perſons, or things, that are indifferent to us.

Friday

Friday 11th. This morning I went to take leave of the chevalier Gluck; and, though it was near eleven o'clock, when I arrived, yet, like a true great genius, he was ftill in bed; *Madame* told me, that he ufually wrote all night, and lay in bed late to recruit. Gluck, when he appeared, did not make fo good a defence but frankly confeffed his fluggifhnefs, *je fuis un peu poltron ce matin.* The niece too was not yet vifible, and the aunt in her defence, faid, that fhe encouraged her fleeping in the morning; *pour fortifier la poitrine,* to ftrengthen the lungs; and, I believe fhe was right, for this excellent little performer is far from robuft.

M. Gluck and I had a long converfation concerning mufical and dramatic effects; concerning *thofe* which had been produced in his *Orfeo* at Vienna ten years ago, when it was firft performed; and three or four years fince, when it was revived at Parma, upon

the

the marriage of the arch-duchess, A-
melia, with the prefent duke; as well as
at Bologna, laft year. He is a great dif-
ciplinarian, and as formidable as Handel
ufed to be, when at the head of a band;
but he affured me, that he never found
his troops mutinous, though he, on no
account, fuffered them to leave any part
of their bufinefs, till it was well done,
and frequently obliged them to repeat
fome of his manœuvres twenty or thirty
times. This was the beft proof he
could give of the wholefomnefs of his
difcipline; for there is a ftrong prefump-
tion, that, when it is endured without
murmur, by men not abfolute flaves to
their commander, they are convinced of
its expediency.

Before we parted, which we did on
very good terms, he furnifhed me with
copies in fcore of his two laft operas of
Alcefte & Paride, and promifed to fend
me a copy of his famous ballet of *Don
Juan*

Juan the next morning; and he kept his word.

From hence I went to Metaſtaſio where I was immediately admitted, though he was in diſhabille, and juſt going to dreſs.

Mademoiſelle Martinetz was at her muſical ſtudies, and writing; ſhe directly complied with my requeſt, of ſitting down to the harpſichord. Metaſtaſio deſired her to ſhew me ſome of her beſt ſtudies; and ſhe produced a pſalm for four voices, with inſtruments. It was a moſt agreeable *Meſcolanza,* as Metaſtaſio called it, of *antico e moderno;* a mixture of the harmony, and contrivance of old times, with the melody and taſte of the preſent. It was an admirable compoſition, and ſhe played and ſung it in a very maſterly manner, contriving ſo well to fill up all the parts, that though it was a full piece, nothing ſeemed wanting. The words of this pſalm were Italian, and of Metaſtaſio's tranſlation.

Z 3　　　　After

After this she obliged me with a
Latin *motet*, for a single voice, which
was grave and solemn, without lan-
guor or heaviness; and then played
me a very pretty harpsichord *sonata* of
her own, which was spirited, and full of
brilliant passages.

I could not finish this visit till I had
petitioned Mademoiselle Martinetz to oblige me with copies of some of her compositions, which she readily granted;
and I had my choice of whatever had
pleased me most among the pieces which
I had heard.

I had the honour of dining with lord
Stormont to-day, for the sixth and last
time, as he was to set out on a journey
at four o'clock the next morning : his
lordship was extremely kind to the last,
offering me letters to Dresden, Berlin,
and Hamburg. The frequent mention
of these honours, will, I fear, have the
appearance of vanity; but a total silence
about

about them, would furely favour of the
worfe vice of ingratitude.

After this I made a fhort vifit to fig-
nor Taruffi, and then a very long one to
Signor Haffe, who to-day read the plan
of my hiftory, in German, with great
attention, and talked over every article
of it with the utmoft cordiality. It
was an infinite fatisfaction to me, I muft
own, to find my ideas fimilar in almoft
all points, to thofe of fuch a man as this;
whofe merit has been univerfally felt,
and is now univerfally allowed.

He faid, that his firft opera was *Antigono*, which he fet, when he was only
eighteen years of age, before he went
into Italy. On his arrival at Naples, he
was thought a very good player on the
harpfichord. He ftudied at firft a little
while under Porpora, as I had been before told by Barbella; but Haffe denied,
that it was Porpora who introduced him
to old Scarlatti. He fays, that the firft
time Scarlatti faw him, he luckily con-

Z 4   ceived

ceived such an affection for him, that
he ever after treated him with the kind-
ness of a father.

When he went back into Germany,
he was taken into the service of the E-
lector of Saxony, who made him set
Antigono again. After this, he set a
German opera, which, with one more,
was all he ever worked upon in that
language.

As he was born near Hamburg, he
told me, that he was not only glad I
was going thither, as it was his country, but, as I should see the great Ema-
nuel Bach there, whom he very much
respected, and hear the best organists and
organs, of any part of the world, unless
they were much degenerated since he
was there. Above all things, he recommended to me the soliciting Bach, to
let me hear him upon the clavichord; and
likewise desired me to enquire after a symphony of that author in E *la mi*, minor,
which he thought the finest he had ever
heard.

I afked him about the difpofition of the orcheftra at Drefden, in 1754, mentioned by Rouffeau in his dictionary, as the beft poffible. He faid, this author's account of it was fo exact, that he fhould fuppofe him to have been there at the time. The king of Poland had then given Haffe unlimited power; and he had every thing of the beft kind, both in vocal and inftrumental mufic, which it was poffible for him to affemble together.

He frequently attended that prince to Warfaw, in Poland, where he compofed feveral operas. He faid the Polifh mufic was truly national, and often very tender and delicate. He mentioned to me a fong which he had made in the Polonoife ftyle, which was one of the moft fingular and the beft received of any one of his compofitions : of this he promifed me a copy, as well as of many other of his moft curious and choice pieces.

In fpeaking of compofers, he commended, the moft of all, old Scarlatti,

and

and Keiſer * : Keiſer, he aſſured me, was,
according to his conceptions, one of the
greateſt muſicians the world ever ſaw.
His compoſitions are more voluminous
than thoſe of old Scarlatti, and his melodies, though more that fifty years old,
are ſuch as would now be thought modern and graceful. This he ſaid had
been always his opinion; and he was not
likely to be biaſſed by prejudice, as this
compoſer was neither his relation, his
maſter, nor even his acquaintance; but
having lately looked at ſome of his works,
he was aſtoniſhed to ſee ſo much more
elegance, clearneſs, and grace, than are
to be found in moſt modern compoſitions, even now. He added, that Keiſer
compoſed chiefly for Hamburg, and,
in general, to the German language.
He was not very well verſed in Italian,
and often blundered in ſetting words; but

* He was born at Weiſſenfels, in Saxony, and
was *maeſtre di capella* to the duke of Mecklenburg.

I   had

had always merit of other kinds to com-
penfate this defect.

He always fpoke refpectfully of Handel, as a player and writer of fugues, as
well as for the ingenuity of his accompaniments, and the natural fimplicity of
his melody, in which particulars he regarded him as the greateft genius that
ever exifted; but faid, that he thought him
too ambitious of difplaying his talent of
working parts and fubjects, as well as too
fond of noife : and Fauftina added, that
his *cantilena* was often rude.

I afked him, if he had ever heard Domenico Scarlatti play? he faid that he had:
as he came from Portugal to Naples, on
a vifit to his father, while he ftudied under him; and he allowed him to have been
poffeffed of a wonderful hand, as well as
fecundity of invention.

He could not think Durante, as a con-
trapuntift, deferved the place which M.
Rouffeau has given him in his dictionary;
but faid that it was old Scarlatti, whom

he

he should have called *le plus grand harmo-
niste d'Italie, c'est à dire du monde*, the
greatest master of harmony of Italy, that
is, of the whole universe; and not Durante, who was not only dry, but *baroque*,
that is, coarse and uncouth *.

He spoke of mademoiselle Martinetz,
as a young person of uncommon talents
for music: said that she sung with great expression, played very neat and masterly,
and was a thorough contrapuntist; but,
added he, " it is pity that her writing
should affect her voice." I had observed,
indeed, the same morning, that she took
the high notes with difficulty. It is an
axiom among all good masters of singing, that stooping to write, and even
sitting much at the harpsichord, hurts
the chest, and greatly affects the voice.

---

* M. Hasse's opinion of Alex. Scarlatti, corres-
ponds exactly with that of Jomelli, who told me, at
Naples, that his compositions for the church, tho'
but little known, were the best of his productions,
and perhaps the best of the kind,

Hasse

Haffe faid, that after he was fifty he had never been able to fing a note; and, indeed he is now fo hoarfe, that he can with difficulty be heard when he fpeaks. This he wholly attributes to his having been fo conftantly employed in writing. Fauftina faid, that when fhe knew him firft, he had a very fine tenor voice; and it was then ufual for mafters to make their fcholars in counterpoint, not only fing, but declaim.

I cannot quit Haffe and Gluck, without faying that it is very neceffary to ufe difcrimination in comparing them together. Haffe may be regarded as the Raphael, and I have already called Gluck the Michael Angelo of living compofers. If the affected French expreffion of *le grand fimple* can ever mean any thing, it muft be when applied to the productions of fuch a compofer as Haffe, who fucceeds better perhaps in expreffing, with clearnefs and propriety, whatever is graceful, elegant, and tender, than what is

boifterous

2

boifterous and violent; whereas Gluck's genius feems more calculated for exciting terror in painting difficult fituations, occafioned by complicated mifery, and the tempeftuous fury of unbridled paffions.

Saturday 12. This morning, after another long vifit to Metaftafio, and hearing mademoifelle Martinetz play and fing with new delight and amazement, I determined to find out the habitation of Vanhall, a young compofer, feveral of whofe productions, particularly his fymphonies, had afforded me fuch uncommon pleafure, that I fhould not hefitate to rank them among the moft complete and perfect compofitions, for many inftruments, which the art of mufic can boaft.

The fpirit of party, in mufical matters, runs high every where; and I every where found that it was wifhed that I fhould hear, or at leaft like, none but the friends of my friends. However, I foon faw, and *heard* through all this, and feldom

dom fuffered myfelf to be the dupe of
partial decifions. For I was not contented with hearing mufic in fine houfes,
theatres, and palaces, but vifited cot-
tages, and garrets, wherever I could get
fcent of a good performer, or a man of
genius.

I had fent my fervant, and made feveral attempts myfelf, to find M. Vanhall before, but in vain. However, to-
day I had been told that he lived without the gates of the city; but, after croff-
ing a branch of the Danube, and walking
feveral miles through a very dufty road,
to the place where I expected to find
him, I was told that he was removed,
no one knew whither: this did not dif-
courage me from enquiring after him
all the way back, and, at length, I luckily
found him, in an obfcure corner of the
town, and in a more lofty than fplendid
fituation. I groped my way up a totally
dark, winding ftone ftair-cafe, at the fummit of which was his bower.

He

He is a civil young man; and though
he could fpeak no French, yet he had a
little Italian, which is the cafe with
many German muficians. I told him
that I was a ftranger, and in queft of
whatever was moft curious in mufic; that
I had heard fome of his fymphonies performed, which had pleafed me very much,
and wifhed to be in poffeffion of a few
of them, if he had any ready tranfcribed,
or if he knew of a copyift who had *.
We foon came to a right underftand-
ing, and finding he played the harpfichord, I got him to fit down to a little
clavichord, and play to me fix leffons
which he had juft made for that inftrument; but I found them neither fo wild
nor fo new as his compofitions for violins.

* As there are no mufic fhops in Vienna, the beft
method of procuring new compofitions, is to apply to
copyifts; for the authors, regarding every Englifh
traveller as a *milord*, expect a prefent on thefe occafions, as confiderable for each piece, as if it had been
compofed on purpofe for him.

Though

Though there have been many admirable compofers of vocal mufic, who, for want of voice, could not *fing*, yet it feems as if it were abfolutely neceffary to be a great *player* on an inftrument in order to write in fuch a manner for it, as will beft fhew its powers. With refpect to the organ and harpfichord, the moft original and ftriking pieces for thofe inftruments have been the productions of great performers, fuch as Handel, Scarlatti, Bach, Schobert, Wagenfeil, Müthel, and Alberti: but a rage for univerfality, or for gain, tempts many compofers to quit the road which nature and art have made familiar to them, for another; in which they are either bewildered or fo deftitute of the neceffary requifites for travelling through it, as to be obliged to rob and plunder every one they meet.

A little perturbation of the faculties, is a promifing circumftance in a young mufician, and M. V. began his career

A a   very

very aufpicioufly, by being fomewhat
flighty. Enthufiafm feems abfolutely
neceffary in all the arts, but particularly
in mufic, which fo much depends upon
fancy and imagination. A cold, fedate,
and wary difpofition, but ill fuits the profeffor of fuch an art; however, when
enthufiafm is ungovernable, and impels
to too frequent and violent efforts, the
intellects are endangered. But as infa-
nity in an artift is fometimes nothing
more than an ebullition of genius, when
that is the cafe, he may cry out to the
phyficians who cure him,

———Pol me occidiftis, amici,
Non fervaftis.

M. V. is now fo far recovered, and
poffeffes a mind fo calm and tranquil, that
his laft pieces appear to me rather infi-
pid and common, and his former agreeable extravagance feems changed into too
great œconomy of thought.

In the afternoon I went to the play, it
was Romeo and Juliet, new written, by
M. Weitz.

M. Weitz. The firſt act was almoſt
over when I arrived; but I ſoon found
that it was not a tranſlation of Shake-
ſpeare; by the ſmall number of characters
in it; there being only eight in this tragedy, and in the Engliſh one of the ſame
name, there are upwards of twenty.

The perſonages introduced by M.
Weitz are Montecute, Capulet, lady Capulet, Romeo, Julie, Laura a Confidant;
inſtead of the Nurſe, Benvoglio a phyſi-
cian; who ſupplies the place of Fryar Law-
rence; and Peter a ſervant to Romeo, inſtead of Balthazar.

Though the ſpeeches and ſcenes were
long; the four firſt acts were very affect-
ing; but the performance both of poet
and actors in the laſt act was abomin-
able. There was no proceſſion; but Juliet, dead at the end of the fourth act, is
found buried at the beginning of the fifth.
The tomb ſcene was bad, ill written and
ill acted; and there was ſo much confuſion,
at laſt, that it was impoſſible to find out

whe-

whether Romeo lived or died. He fwallowed poifon, indeed, which had racked, tortured and deprived him of his fenfes; but, as the doctor plied him well with drops, and a fmelling bottle, he recovered juft enough to fay Juliet!—oh my Juliet! Julie! Oh meine Julie! and the curtain dropped.

Sunday 13th. There was a proceffion through the principal ftreets of this city to day, as an anniverfary commemoration of the Turks having been driven from its walls in 1683, by Sobiefki king of Poland, after it had fuftained a fiege of two months. The Emperor came from Laxemberg to attend the celebration of this feftival, and walked in the proceffion, which fet off from the Francifcan's church, and proceeded through the principal ftreets of the city to the Cathedral of St. Stephen, where *Te Deum* was fung, under the direction of M. Gafman, imperial *maeftro di capella*. The mufic was by Reüter,

I an

an old German compofer, without tafte
or invention. As there was a very numerous band, great noife and little meaning characterized the whole performance. I hoped fomething better would
have fucceeded this dull, dry ftuff; but
what followed was equally uninterefting.
The whole was finifhed by a triple dif-
charge of all the artillery of the city,
and the military inftruments were little
lefs noify now, than the mufical had been
before.

From hence I went to Metaftafio, for
the laft time! I found with him much
company, and the St. Cecilia Martinetz at
the harpfichord, to which fhe had been
finging. At her defire there was a com-
mutation of compofitions between us.
She had been fo kind as to have tranfcribed for me, among other things, a
fong of Metaftafio, fet by herfelf, with
which I had been greatly ftruck in a former vifit.

A a 3

The

The good old poet embraced me heartily; said he was sorry to lose me so soon; that he must have my book, when published, and defired to hear from me. Thus we parted at Vienna; but I cannot quit him here, without adding a few lines to this article, long as it is already.

I had been told, and it was likewise the opinion of Signor Haffe, that Metaftafio had more of his own manufcript poetry in his poffeffion, than had hitherto been publifhed; but lord Stormont doubts much of the fact; alledging his principle of never working but when he is called upon, againft his writing verfes merely to lock them up. Metaftafio laughs at all poetic infpiration, and makes a poem as mechanically as another would make a fhoe, at what time he pleafes, and with-out any other occafion than the want of it.

However, lord Stormont fays, that he has feen a tranflation of Horace's *Ars Poetica,*

in

in Italian verfe, by Metaftafio, which he thinks far fuperior to every one that has been made in other languages. He has likewife tranflated the *Hoc erat in votis,* of the fame poet, admirably well. In this, like Horace, he has told the ftory of the Town and Country Moufe, as a ferious fact, and kept more clofely, both to the letter and fpirit of the original, than any other who has hitherto attempted it.

Metaftafio, like moft other perfons in years, has an averfion to the talking about his own age, about the infirmities of his friends, or the calamities, or death, even of perfons that are indifferent to him. He is extremely candid in his judgment of men of genius, and even of poets with whom he has had a difference, which indeed are very few. For, when he has been attacked by them, it has often happened, that, after writing an epigram or couplet, to fhew his particular friends how he could defend him-

felf,

felf, he has thrown it into the fire; and he has never been known either to print or publifh a line, by way of retaliation, againft the bitteref enemy to his perfon or poems.

He has a natural chearfulnefs and pleafantry, in his manner and converfation, which give a gaiety to all around him; and is poffeffed of as eafy an eloquence in fpeaking as in writing. He is, indeed, one of the few extraordinary geniufes who lofe nothing by approximation or acquaintance: for, it is a melancholy reflection that, very few, like him, are equally intitled to the epithets *good* and *great*.

The following anecdote has been given me by a perfon of veracity, well informed of every particular, relative to this great poet. Many years ago, when Metaftafio's circumftances were far from affluent, and he was only known at Vienna as an affiftant writer for the Opera, under Apoftolo Zeno; a perfon with
whom

whom he had contracted a great intimacy and friendſhip, dying, left him his whole fortune, amounting to fifteen thouſand pounds ſterling. But Metaſtaſio hearing that he had relations at Bologna, went thither in ſearch of them; and having found ſuch as he thought beſt intitled to theſe poſſeſſions, told them, that though his deceaſed friend had bequeathed to him his whole fortune, he could ſuppoſe it to be no otherwiſe than in truſt, till he ſhould find out the moſt deſerving of his kindred, in order to divide it equitably among them; which he immediately did, without the leaſt reſerve in his own favour.

After dinner, I had the pleaſure of a long viſit from M. Gaſman, who not only furniſhed me with a liſt of his works, but obliged me with copies of a great number of his manuſcript quartets, for various inſtruments *. M.

* It is but juſtice to ſay, that ſince my return to England, I have had theſe pieces tried, and have
found

Gafman is of a middle age, and yet his works are very voluminous. For the ferious opera, he has compofed, in Italy, *Merope, Iffipile, Catone in Utica, Ezio,* twice, and *Achille in Sciro.* At Vienna, *Olimpiade, Amore di Pfiche,* and *Il Trionfo d'Amore.* For the comic opera, at Venice, *l'Uccilatore,* twice: *il Filofofo inamorato, un Pazzo ne fa Cento,* and *il Mondo nella Luna.* At Vienna, *i Viaggiatori ridicoli, l'Amore Artigiano, la Notte Critica, l'opera Seria, la Conteffina, il Filofofo inamorato* a fecond time, *la Pefcatrice,* and *i Rovinati.*

When M. Gafman left me, I went, for the laft time, to M. Wagenfeil, and heard him and his little female fcholar play feveral brilliant duets upon two harpfichords: here I again met with my

found them excellent: there is pleafing melody, free from caprice and affectation; found harmony, and the contrivances and imitations are ingenious, without the leaft confufion. In fhort, the ftyle is fober and fedate, without dulnefs; and mafterly, without pedantry.

friend

friend, the Portuguese Abbé, and, after a long converfation upon mufical matters, we parted; but not till we had mutual-ly exchanged directions, and promifes to keep alive our friendfhip, by a literary intercourfe.

After this I flew home, to pack, and to pay; here, among other things, I was plagued with copyifts the whole evening; they began to regard me as a greedy and indifcriminate purchafer of whatever trafh they fhould offer; but I was forced to hold my hand, not only from buying bad mufic, but good. For every thing is very dear at Vienna, and nothing more fo than mufic, of which none is printed.

As it was, I did not quit Vienna till I had expended ten or twelve guineas in the purchafe of mufic; which, with what had been given me, what I had tran-fcribed myfelf, and the printed books I had collected, rendered my baggage fo unwieldy, as to coft me an additional

horfe

horfe to my chaife, all the way to Hamburg.

. Indeed, Vienna is fo rich in compofers,
and inclofes within its walls fuch a number of muficians of fuperior merit, that,
it is but juft to allow it to be, among
German cities, the imperial feat of mufic, as well as of power.

This might be manifefted by a recapi-
tulation of what I heard, and faw, during
my fhort refidence there ; but I fhall
leave that to the reader's recollection,
and only mention the names of Haffe,
Gluck, Gafman, Wagenfeil, Salieri, Hofman, Haydn, Ditters, Vanhall, and Huber, who have all greatly diftinguifhed
themfelves as compofers ; and the fymphonies and quartets of the five laft mentioned authors, are perhaps among the
firft full pieces and compofitions, for
violins, that have ever been produced.

To thefe celebrated names, may be
added thofe of Mifliwiceck, a Bohemian,

juft

just returned from Italy, where he has established a great reputation by his operas, as well as instrumental music; Scarlatti, nephew to the famous Domenico Scarlatti; Kohaut, an excellent lutanist; Venturini, a hautbois player of the first class; Albrechtzberger, and Stefani, two eminent harpsichord players, in the service of the court, and La Motte, a Flamand, the best solo player and sightsman, upon the violin, at Vienna. He was some time scholar to Giardini; and it is related of him, that when he quitted his first master, he travelled through Italy, still in search of another; and being arrived at Leghorn, where Nardini then lived, he would have become his scholar; but after hearing that performer execute one of his own solos, of the most difficult kind, and being, in his turn asked to play, he desired leave to perform the same solo, which he had just heard, and which was new, and in manuscript, so that he never could have practised it; how-

however, he acquitted himfelf fo well,
that Nardini declined taking as a *fcholar*,
one who was already fo able a mafter of
his inftrument.

I omit particularizing here, all the able
organifts of this city, the *dilettanti*, male
and female, and the feveral mafters and
performers, vocal and inftrumental, who
conftantly refide here; and contribute to
the cultivation of mufic; and the pleafure
of its votaries and protectors; and fhall
only remark that, rich as this city is at
prefent, in muficians of genius and eminence, there is no ferious opera either at
the court or public theatre.

Lady Mary Wortley Montague men-
tions an opera that was performed in the
open air, when fhe was at Vienna, the
decorations and habits of which coft the
emperor thirty thoufand pounds fterling;
and, during the reigns of the late emperors, from the firft years of Leopold,
to the middle of the prefent century,
there ufed to be operas at the expence of
the

the court, written, compofed, and performed, by perfons of the greateft abilities that could be affembled from all
parts of Europe : but the frequent wars,
and other calamities of this country, have
fo exhaufted the public treafure, and im-
poverifhed individuals, that this expenfive
cuftom is now,

    " To my mind,
" More honoured in the breach, than the obferv-
    ance,"

For though I love mufic very well, yet I
love humanity better.

END OF THE FIRST VOLUME.

I N D E X.

Colista,

Hofmann,

M.

MAESTRICK, 63.

Mancini, Signor, finging-mafter at Vienna, 324, 332.

MANHEIM, 80.

Manfervifi, Signora, finger at Munich, 147.

Marmontel, his Zemire and Azor, 23.

Martinetz, M. librarian at Vienna, 317.

————— Mademoifelle, 306, 341, 348, 350, 358.

Martini, Padre, 127.

Metaftafio Signor Abate, 223. Sketch of his life, 224. Diflike of extempore verfes, 225. Not partial to the ancients, opinion of blank verfe, 226. His regular life, 227, 245. Vifited by the author, 293, 305, 341, 358. Laughs at poetic infpiration, 359. Inftance of generofity, 361.

Meyer, organ builder, 74.

Michel, compofer, 170.

Migliavacca, 306.

Millico, Signor, 259.

Minelli, Giorgio Battifta, 334.

Mingotti, Signora, 123, 142. Sketch of her life, 150, 169, 173, 236.

Mifliwiceck, compofer, 365.

Mittermeir, organift at Vienna, 239.

Mozart, 126.

Montague, lady M. W. her account of the theatre at Vienna, 211, 366.

MUNICH, 121, 142.

Mufic, military, in France, 5, 6, 10. At Ghent, 17. At Darmftadt, 77. At Manheim, 80.

Mut, performer on the harp at Vienna, 279.

Müthel, compofer, 353.

N.

Nardini, 104, 365.

National mufic, 108, 202, 249.

Naumann, *maeftro di capella* of the Elector of Bavaria, 130, 138.

Newton, father, 32, 45, 46.

Noverre, M. ballet-mafter at Vienna, 220.

NYMPHENBURG, 130, 166.

O.

OMER'S, ST. 1.

※

Music and Books published by Travis & Emery Music Bookshop:

Anon.: Hymnarium Sarisburiense, cum Rubricis et Notis Musicis.

Agricola, Johann Friedrich from Tosi: Anleitung zur Singkunst.

Bach, C.P.E.: edited W. Emery: Nekrolog or Obituary Notice of J.S. Bach.

Bateson, Naomi Judith: Alcock of Salisbury

Bathe, William: A Briefe Introduction to the Skill of Song

Bax, Arnold: Symphony #5, Arranged for Piano Four Hands by Walter Emery

Burney, Charles: The Present State of Music in France and Italy

Burney, Charles: The Present State of Music in Germany, The Netherlands ...

Burney, Charles: An Account of the Musical Performances ... Handel

Burney, Karl: Nachricht von Georg Friedrich Handel's Lebensumstanden.

Burns, Robert: The Caledonian Musical Museum ..The Best Scotch Songs. (1810)

Cobbett, W.W.: Cobbett's Cyclopedic Survey of Chamber Music. (2 vols.)

Corrette, Michel: Le Maitre de Clavecin

Crimp, Bryan: Dear Mr. Rosenthal ... Dear Mr. Gaisberg ...

Crimp, Bryan: Solo: The Biography of Solomon

d'Indy, Vincent: Beethoven: Biographie Critique

d'Indy, Vincent: Beethoven: A Critical Biography

d'Indy, Vincent: César Franck (in French)

Fischhof, Joseph: Versuch einer Geschichte des Clavierbaues. (Faksimile 1853).

Frescobaldi, Girolamo: D'Arie Musicali per Cantarsi. Primo & Secondo Libro.

Geminiani, Francesco: The Art of Playing the Violin.

Handel; Purcell; Boyce; Geene et al: Calliope or English Harmony: Volume First.

Häuser: Musikalisches Lexikon. 2 vols in one.

Hawkins, John: A General History of the Science and Practice of Music (5 vols.)

Herbert-Caesari, Edgar: The Science and Sensations of Vocal Tone

Herbert-Caesari, Edgar: Vocal Truth

Hopkins and Rimboult: The Organ. Its History and Construction.

Hunt, John: - see separate list of discographies at the end of these titles

Isaacs, Lewis: Hänsel and Gretel. A Guide to Humperdinck's Opera.

Isaacs, Lewis: Königskinder (Royal Children) A Guide to Humperdinck's Opera.

Kastner: Manuel Général de Musique Militaire

Lacassagne, M. l'Abbé Joseph : Traité Général des élémens du Chant.

Lascelles (née Catley), Anne: The Life of Miss Anne Catley.

Mainwaring, John: Memoirs of the Life of the Late George Frederic Handel

Malcolm, Alexander: A Treaty of Music: Speculative, Practical and Historical

Marx, Adolph Bernhard: Die Kunst des Gesanges, Theoretisch-Practisch

May, Florence: The Life of Brahms

May, Florence: The Girlhood Of Clara Schumann: Clara Wieck And Her Time.

Mellers, Wilfrid: Angels of the Night: Popular Female Singers of Our Time

Mellers, Wilfrid: Bach and the Dance of God

Mellers, Wilfrid: Beethoven and the Voice of God

Mellers, Wilfrid: Caliban Reborn - Renewal in Twentieth Century Music

Music and Books published by Travis & Emery Music Bookshop:

Mellers, Wilfrid: Darker Shade of Pale, A Backdrop to Bob Dylan
Mellers, Wilfrid: François Couperin and the French Classical Tradition
Mellers, Wilfrid: Harmonious Meeting
Mellers, Wilfrid: Le Jardin Retrouvé, The Music of Frederic Mompou
Mellers, Wilfrid: Music and Society, England and the European Tradition
Mellers, Wilfrid: Music in a New Found Land: ... ... American Music
Mellers, Wilfrid: Romanticism and the Twentieth Century (from 1800)
Mellers, Wilfrid: The Masks of Orpheus: ...... the Story of European Music.
Mellers, Wilfrid: The Sonata Principle (from c. 1750)
Mellers, Wilfrid: Vaughan Williams and the Vision of Albion
Panchianio, Cattuffio: Rutzvanscad Il Giovine
Pearce, Charles: Sims Reeves, Fifty Years of Music in England.
Playford, John: An Introduction to the Skill of Musick.
Purcell, Henry et al: Harmonia Sacra ... The First Book, (1726)
Purcell, Henry et al: Harmonia Sacra ... Book II (1726)
Quantz, Johann: Versuch einer Anweisung die Flöte trave   rsiere zu spielen.
Rameau, Jean-Philippe: Code de Musique Pratique, ou Methodes.
Rastall, Richard: The Notation of Western Music.
Rimbault, Edward: The Pianoforte, Its Origins, Progress, and Construction.
Rousseau, Jean Jacques: Dictionnaire de Musique
Rubinstein, Anton : Guide to the proper use of the Pianoforte Pedals.
Sainsbury, John S.: Dictionary of Musicians. (1825). 2 vols.
Serré de Rieux, Jean de : Les dons des Enfans de Latone
Simpson, Christopher: A Compendium of Practical Musick in Five Parts
Spohr, Louis: Autobiography
Spohr, Louis: Grand Violin School
Tans'ur, William: A New Musical Grammar; or The Harmonical Spectator
Terry, Charles Sanford: Bach's Chorals – Parts 1, 2 and 3.
Terry, Charles Sanford: John Christian Bach
Terry, Charles Sanford: J.S. Bach's Original Hymn-Tunes for Congregational Use.
Terry, Charles Sanford: Four-Part Chorals of J.S. Bach. (German & English)
Terry, Charles Sanford: Joh. Seb. Bach, Cantata Texts, Sacred and Secular.
Terry, Charles Sanford: The Origins of the Family of Bach Musicians.
Tosi, Pierfrancesco: Opinioni de' Cantori Antichi, e Moderni
Tosi, Pierfrancesco: Observations on the Florid Song.
Van der Straeten, Edmund: History of the Violoncello, The Viol da Gamba ...
Van der Straeten, Edmund: History of the Violin, Its Ancestors... (2 vols.)
Walther, J. G. [Waltern]: Musicalisches Lexikon [Musikalisches Lexicon]
Zwirn, Gerald: Stranded Stories From The Operas

Travis & Emery Music Bookshop
17 Cecil Court, London, WC2N 4EZ, United Kingdom.
Tel. (+44) 20 7240 2129

© Travis & Emery 2010

Discographies by Travis & Emery:

Discographies by John Hunt.

1987: 978-1-906857-14-1: From Adam to Webern: the Recordings of von Karajan.

1991: 978-0-951026-83-0: 3 Italian Conductors and 7 Viennese Sopranos: 10 Discographies: Arturo Toscanini, Guido Cantelli, Carlo Maria Giulini, Elisabeth Schwarzkopf, Irmgard Seefried, Elisabeth Gruemmer, Sena Jurinac, Hilde Gueden, Lisa Della Casa, Rita Streich.

1992: 978-0-951026-85-4: Mid-Century Conductors and More Viennese Singers: 10 Discographies: Karl Boehm, Victor De Sabata, Hans Knappertsbusch, Tullio Serafin, Clemens Krauss, Anton Dermota, Leonie Rysanek, Eberhard Waechter, Maria Reining, Erich Kunz.

1993: 978-0-951026-87-8: More 20th Century Conductors: 7 Discographies: Eugen Jochum, Ferenc Fricsay, Carl Schuricht, Felix Weingartner, Josef Krips, Otto Klemperer, Erich Kleiber.

1994: 978-0-951026-88-5: Giants of the Keyboard: 6 Discographies: Wilhelm Kempff, Walter Gieseking, Edwin Fischer, Clara Haskil, Wilhelm Backhaus, Artur Schnabel.

1994: 978-0-951026-89-2: Six Wagnerian Sopranos: 6 Discographies: Frieda Leider, Kirsten Flagstad, Astrid Varnay, Martha Moedl, Birgit Nilsson, Gwyneth Jones.

1995: 978-0-952582-70-0: Musical Knights: 6 Discographies: Henry Wood, Thomas Beecham, Adrian Boult, John Barbirolli, Reginald Goodall, Malcolm Sargent.

1995: 978-0-952582-71-7: A Notable Quartet: 4 Discographies: Gundula Janowitz, Christa Ludwig, Nicolai Gedda, Dietrich Fischer-Dieskau.

1996: 978-0-952582-75-5: Leopold Stokowski (1882-1977): Discography and Concert Register

1996: 978-0-952582-76-2: Makers of the Philharmonia: 11 Discographies: Alceo Galliera, Walter Susskind, Paul Kletzki, Nicolai Malko, Issay Dobrowen, Lovro Von Matacic, Efrem Kurtz, Otto Ackermann, Anatole Fistoulari, George Weldon, Robert Irving.

1996: 978-0-952582-72-4: The Post-War German Tradition: 5 Discographies: Rudolf Kempe, Joseph Keilberth, Wolfgang Sawallisch, Rafael Kubelik, Andre Cluytens.

1996: 978-0-952582-73-1: Teachers and Pupils: 7 Discographies: Elisabeth Schwarzkopf, Maria Ivoguen, Maria Cebotari, Meta Seinemeyer, Ljuba Welitsch, Rita Streich, Erna Berger.

1996: 978-0-952582-75-5: Leopold Stokowski: Discography and Concert Listing.

1996: 978-0-952582-76-2: Makers of the Philharmonia: 11 Discographies Alceo Galliera, Walter Susskind, Paul Kletzki, Nicolai Malko, Issay Dobrowen, Lovro Von Matacic, Efrem Kurtz, Otto Ackermann, Anatole Fistoulari, George Weldon, Robert Irving.

1996: 978-0-952582-77-9: Tenors in a Lyric Tradition: 3 Discographies: Peter Anders, Walther Ludwig, Fritz Wunderlich.

1997: 978-0-952582-78-6: The Lyric Baritone: 5 Discographies: Hans Reinmar, Gerhard Huesch, Josef Metternich, Hermann Uhde, Eberhard Waechter.

1997: 978-0-952582-79-3: Hungarians in Exile: 3 Discographies: Fritz Reiner, Antal Dorati, George Szell.

1997: 978-1-901395-00-6: The Art of the Diva: 3 Discographies: Claudia Muzio, Maria Callas, Magda Olivero.

1997: 978-1-901395-01-3: Metropolitan Sopranos: 4 Discographies: Rosa Ponselle, Eleanor Steber, Zinka Milanov, Leontyne Price.

1997: 978-1-901395-02-0: Back From The Shadows: 4 Discographies: Willem Mengelberg, Dimitri Mitropoulos, Hermann Abendroth, Eduard Van Beinum.

1997: 978-1-901395-03-7: More Musical Knights: 4 Discographies: Hamilton Harty, Charles Mackerras, Simon Rattle, John Pritchard.

1998: 978-1-901395-95-2: More Giants of the Keyboard: 5 Discographies: Claudio Arrau, Gyorgy Cziffra, Vladimir Horowitz, Dinu Lipatti, Artur Rubinstein.

1998: 978-1-901395-94-5: Conductors On The Yellow Label: 8 Discographies: Fritz Lehmann, Ferdinand Leitner, Ferenc Fricsay, Eugen Jochum, Leopold Ludwig, Artur Rother, Franz Konwitschny, Igor Markevitch.

1998: 978-1-901395-96-9: Mezzo and Contraltos: 5 Discographies: Janet Baker, Margarete Klose, Kathleen Ferrier, Giulietta Simionato, Elisabeth Hoengen.

1999: 978-1-901395-97-6: The Furtwaengler Sound Sixth Edition: Discography and Concert Listing.

1999: 978-1-901395-98-3: The Great Dictators: 3 Discographies: Evgeny Mravinsky, Artur Rodzinski, Sergiu Celibidache.

1999: 978-1-901395-99-0: Sviatoslav Richter: Pianist of the Century: Discography.

2000: 978-1-901395-04-4: Philharmonic Autocrat 1: Discography of: Herbert Von Karajan [Third Edition].

2000: 978-1-901395-05-1: Wiener Philharmoniker 1 - Vienna Philharmonic and Vienna State Opera Orchestras: Discography Part 1 1905-1954.

2000: 978-1-901395-06-8: Wiener Philharmoniker 2 - Vienna Philharmonic and Vienna State Opera Orchestras: Discography Part 2 1954-1989.

2001: 978-1-901395-07-5: Gramophone Stalwarts: 3 Separate Discographies: Bruno Walter, Erich Leinsdorf, Georg Solti.

2001: 978-1-901395-08-2: Singers of the Third Reich: 5 Discographies: Helge Roswaenge, Tiana Lemnitz, Franz Voelker, Maria Mueller, Max Lorenz.

2001: 978-1-901395-09-9: Philharmonic Autocrat 2: Concert Register of Herbert Von Karajan Second Edition.

2002: 978-1-901395-10-5: Sächsische Staatskapelle Dresden: Complete Discography.

2002: 978-1-901395-11-2: Carlo Maria Giulini: Discography and Concert Register.

2002: 978-1-901395-12-9: Pianists For The Connoisseur: 6 Discographies: Arturo Benedetti Michelangeli, Alfred Cortot, Alexis Weissenberg, Clifford Curzon, Solomon, Elly Ney.

2003: 978-1-901395-14-3: Singers on the Yellow Label: 7 Discographies: Maria Stader, Elfriede Troetschel, Annelies Kupper, Wolfgang Windgassen, Ernst Haefliger, Josef Greindl, Kim Borg.

2003: 978-1-901395-15-0: A Gallic Trio: 3 Discographies: Charles Muench, Paul Paray, Pierre Monteux.

2004: 978-1-901395-16-7: Antal Dorati 1906-1988: Discography and Concert Register.

2004: 978-1-901395-17-4: Columbia 33CX Label Discography.

2004: 978-1-901395-18-1: Great Violinists: 3 Discographies: David Oistrakh, Wolfgang Schneiderhan, Arthur Grumiaux.

2006: 978-1-901395-19-8: Leopold Stokowski: Second Edition of the Discography.

2006: 978-1-901395-20-4: Wagner Im Festspielhaus: Discography of the Bayreuth Festival.

2006: 978-1-901395-21-1: Her Master's Voice: Concert Register and Discography of Dame Elisabeth Schwarzkopf [Third Edition].

2007: 978-1-901395-22-8: Hans Knappertsbusch: Kna: Concert Register and Discography of Hans Knappertsbusch, 1888-1965. Second Edition.

2008: 978-1-901395-23-5: Philips Minigroove: Second Extended Version of the European Discography.

2009: 978-1-901395-24-2: American Classics: The Discographies of Leonard Bernstein and Eugene Ormandy.

2010: 978-1-901395-25-9: Dirigenten der DDR: Conductors of the German Democratic Republic

Discography by Stephen J. Pettitt, edited by John Hunt:
1987: 978-1-906857-16-5: Philharmonia Orchestra: Complete Discography 1945-1987

Available from: Travis & Emery at 17 Cecil Court, London, UK.
(+44) 20 7 240 2129. email on sales@travis-and-emery.com .

www.ingramcontent.com/pod-product-compliance
Lightning Source LLC
Chambersburg PA
CBHW060238100426
42742CB00011B/1572